HIDDEN
HISTORY
of
CLEMSON
FOOTBALL

HIDDEN
HISTORY
of
CLEMSON
FOOTBALL

Will Vandervort

THE
History
PRESS

Published by The History Press
Charleston, SC
www.historypress.com

Front cover: Clemson Athletic Communications.
Back cover: Clemson Athletic Communications; *inset*: *The Clemson Insider*.

First published 2020

Manufactured in the United States

ISBN 9781467143493

Library of Congress Control Number: 2020938438

CONTENTS

Contents

ACKNOWLEDGEMENTS

I remember it like it was yesterday. I was four years old, and I was riding with my stepdad in the front seat of his car. This was in the late 1970s, and back then, children, no matter their age or height, were allowed to ride in the front seat. We weren't even required to wear a seat belt. Most of the time, at that age, I was standing on the front seat.

But getting back to the story. I remember my stepdad had a car console in the middle of the front floor. Back then, consoles were not built into cars like they are now. In those days, you went to an Auto Zone or K-Mart and you purchased one, usually for less than ten dollars.

In the middle of the console was a place to put anything you wanted… snacks, receipts or football tickets. On this particular day, my stepdad had two Clemson football tickets sitting in the console. At the time, I did not know what they were. I did not know anything about football. On the front of the ticket was Clemson's signature orange helmet with the white tiger paw.

The tiger paw intrigued me. I did not know what it was, so I asked him. "Carl! What's that?" I asked.

He looked at me puzzled and looked down to where I was pointing and smiled. "Those are my Clemson tickets for this Saturday's football game. Me and your Uncle Billie are going," he said.

I had no idea what he was talking about. But I was fascinated by the tiger paw. It is a very vivid memory I have. To be honest, it is one of the first from my childhood. Little did I know that tiger paw was going to become so influential in my life.

Since I could remember, I was a Clemson fan. Though my father was born and raised in Pittsburgh and my mother went to Furman, I was raised a Clemson fan. Mom loved her Tigers. She was born and raised in Greenville, South Carolina, and listened to her Tigers play every week. My oldest brother, Don, who is twelve years older than me, worked at WFBC Radio in Greenville and was friends with Jim Phillips, the voice of the Tigers for thirty-six years until his unexpected death in 2003.

My stepdad, of course, was a Clemson graduate. He graduated from Clemson College in 1949. He was a cadet and attended school there on the GI Bill after he got back from World War II.

Carl taught me everything about Clemson. How it was started, why it was a military school and its military heritage. He loved Clemson and passed that love on to me.

I was obsessed with Clemson sports growing up, in particular Clemson football. I grew up in a great era for Clemson football. By the time I was old enough to know what was going on, the Tigers were having their greatest run.

The first season I can really remember was the 1981 season. What a great season to remember, right? I remember it all so clearly. Literally, like it was yesterday. I was just nine years old, and my entire wardrobe was orange. I wore a Clemson T-shirt every day to school. I even had orange-and-white Converses, and I would only wear white socks that had orange stripes on them.

Mom encouraged my obsession. We listened to every game together in 1981. It was truly a magical season. I remember every big play from the season and where I was and what I was doing when the final seconds ticked down in the 1982 Orange Bowl as the Tigers' wrapped up the 1981 national championship.

At the time, I thought this was what life was as a Clemson fan. You celebrated a lot and you won championships. What a great year to be a Tiger!

By the time I was twelve, I was all in. My brother would bring me all the game notes, media and bowl guides. I read them more than I read my textbooks in school. Ask my teachers, they will tell you.

This is how I became a nerd when it came to Clemson football. Now, I am no Tim Bourret or Sam Blackman. They know Clemson history better than any two people I know. Of course, they learned from the master, longtime sports information director Bob Bradley, who passed away in 2000.

I learned from Mr. Bradley, too, but not directly. I learned from reading all of his game notes and media guides. I was thirsty for Clemson sports knowledge, and those three guys, unknowingly, quenched my thirst.

It was about that time that I knew what I wanted to do for a living. I wanted to do something in the sports field. I didn't know exactly what, but I knew I wanted to work in the industry full time. It was my passion, and it still is.

As you know, I eventually became a sportswriter and, by God's hands, I found myself covering Clemson football and Clemson athletics on a daily basis. It was never my intention to cover Clemson athletics when I got in the business, but it is where God led me.

When I was in the sixth grade, our English teacher gave us an assignment. She wanted us to write a small book about what we enjoy the most in life. Of course, most of my friends wrote about going hunting with their dads, playing baseball, fishing, riding their bikes—you get the point. As for me, I wrote about Clemson football, particularly the history of Clemson football.

I still have that book. Technically, it's the first one I wrote. By the way, in case you are wondering, I got an A.

There are a lot of people I want to thank for allowing one of my passions to come to life. First, my late parents. My dad got me hooked on sports and introduced me to my beloved Pittsburgh Steelers. My stepdad, as I mentioned, introduced me to Clemson. I am forever grateful that he introduced me to what I believe is one of the best places on earth.

My mom and I spent many days and countless hours listening to the Tigers play. If I did not attend a game, she and I listened to every Jim Phillips call. We did that until the day I went off to college. My mom was my biggest fan and encouraged me from the time I was a little boy to be whatever I wanted to be. She never discouraged me from doing my stats, acting like I was broadcasting games, making my own top 25 polls or watching or listening to football every Saturday and Sunday. She let me be me. Thanks, Mom!

I want to acknowledge my brother Kevin. Since Mom passed away, he became my biggest fan. He lifts me up when I am down, and he stayed on me until I completed this book. He is my best friend, and I am so thankful for him.

I want to thank all the people who helped with interviews, research, pictures, all of it: Joanne Bethea, Bart Boatwright, Rex Brown, Gavin Oliver, Brian Hennessy, Jeff Kalin, Phil Sikes, George Bennett and my boss at *The Clemson Insider*, Robert MacRae.

I want to thank Chad Rhoad of The History Press for being so patient. With Clemson making another run at a national championship, writing this book was not easy. Chad was great, and I appreciate all of his efforts.

Thank you to former Clemson sports information director Tim Bourret and former assistant sports information director Sam Blackman for being so great as always in interviews and helping with information and research. I want to thank Clemson football communications director Ross Taylor, as well, for setting up interviews.

Thank you to the former players and coaches, like C.J. Spiller, Steve Fuller, Danny Ford, Bill D'Andrea, Terry Don Phillips, Jeff Davis, Homer Jordan and the list goes on and on, for being so gracious and speaking with me during this project.

Finally, thank you to Coach Dabo Swinney for allowing me the opportunity to speak not only with him but also to his players and coaches and for giving me and the rest of the media the access we need to do our jobs on a daily basis, so that stories can be told and written and used in a history book about one of the best programs in all of college football.

—Will Vandervort
January 31, 2020

INTRODUCTION

When you walk into Dabo Swinney's office at the Allen Reeves Football Complex, it's like walking into a museum—a Clemson football museum, that is. Swinney has just about everything in there. Memorabilia from Clemson's three national championships and autographed footballs from Clemson legends and college football dignitaries, as well as things that only have a personal connection to him.

His most prized possession sits on his desk: a glass paperweight with a business card inside. On the back of the business card is a written agreement between Swinney and former Clemson running back C.J. Spiller. It reads, "I, C.J. Spiller, agree to visit CU on the 13th of Jan. 06."

It was an informal contract Swinney made on the spot when he visited Spiller in Lake Butler, Florida, on a recruiting trip in 2005 to see linebacker Kevin Alexander, a high school teammate of Spiller's who had already committed to Clemson. Swinney, then the wide receivers' coach at Clemson, knew Spiller was a man of his word and that drawing up this impromptu contract would guarantee the five-star running back was going to come and visit Clemson at the very least.

"I did not know much about Clemson. I knew of Clemson because I grew up a Florida State fan and those teams played each other every year," Spiller said. "So, I kind of knew the team, but I did not know in depth what the program was all about.

"Every time Coach Swinney would come down to see Kevin, I used to see him in our football building. So, one day, I came over and introduced myself to him. He said, 'I know who you are.' He said it in his typical Coach Swinney fashion. I think the conversations just started from there. He kept coming back and coming back. I had four schools solid that I was going to visit, so I only had one visit remaining. Ironically, it came down between Clemson and Alabama."

Spiller kept his commitment and visited Clemson on January 13, 2006. Three weeks later, he slipped his mother, Patricia Watkins, a note as he walked to the podium to make his announcement on where he was planning to play college football. "She was a huge Florida fan, and rightfully so," Spiller said. "Coach [Urban] Meyer came in and did his sweettalk to her and, obviously, being a mom, she wanted me to be close to home. She wasn't sure about Clemson. She did not know. She had never been to Clemson. She went to Florida State with me. She did not go to Miami or Southern Cal, but she went to Florida with me. So, she kind of knew what those two programs were about with Florida State and Florida. She had no idea with Clemson. All she knew was the hearsay from what the coaches told her and so that kind of made her angry."

Then in front of all of his high school peers and an auditorium full of Florida fans, Spiller told them he was coming to Clemson. As you can imagine, everyone was in shock. "You could hear a pin drop in there. It just went completely silent....It was a lot of pressure, but I knew I had to do what was best for me. When you go back and watch the tape of me signing my letter of intent, Mom was really angry," Spiller said.

The rest is history, you might say. Spiller ultimately made the right choice, as he broke countless Clemson and ACC records and even a few NCAA records in his four years in Tigertown. But what the running back and former ACC Player of the Year actually did was greater than any of those things. Because he took a chance to come to a school that had not won much of anything in the two decades prior to his arrival, Spiller changed the Clemson football program, much like Steve Fuller did in 1975 when he picked Clemson over Georgia and Tennessee.

Fuller's presence and the amount of success he was able to have at Clemson allowed other top athletes to believe the same could happen for them at Clemson. Eventually, the Tigers were signing some of the best players in the country, and the results showed on the football field. From 1977 to 1991, Clemson won 133 games, did not have a losing record for fifteen straight seasons, won seven ACC Championships, appeared in eleven bowl games, won seven bowl games, recorded six ten-win seasons and, most important, won the program's first national championship in 1981.

Above: Banks McFadden (66) was an All-American for Clemson in 1939, leading the Tigers to their first bowl game at the end of the season. *Clemson Athletic Communications.*

Right: All-American Banks McFadden. He is still considered Clemson's greatest athlete. *Clemson Athletic Communications.*

Clemson had seen such acts before in its lustrous history. Fred Cone, whom Frank Howard called his greatest player, had the same effect in the late 1940s, which began a decade that saw the Tigers post a perfect season in 1948, win three ACC Championships, play in six bowl games, winning three of them.

Before Cone, there was Banks McFadden, who led Clemson to the program's first bowl appearance and victory following the 1939 season. An All-American in football, basketball and track, McFadden is still considered the greatest athlete to play at Clemson.

These days, even though it's been ten years since he last wore a Clemson uniform, Tiger fans are still seeing the benefits of Spiller's legacy. Clemson legends like Tajh Boyd, Deandre Hopkins, Sammy Watkins, Deshaun Watson and countless others have said Spiller's success at Clemson played a big role in why they chose to come to Clemson.

After Spiller put on the orange and white in 2006, and through the 2019 season, the Tigers won 150 games. They won two national championships and played for it two other times. They won six ACC Championships, played in 18 bowl games (including 4 national championship games) and made the College Football Playoff five times.

Spiller was picked ninth overall in the 2009 NFL draft, and through the 2019 draft, ten other former Tigers have followed the same path.

Swinney's business card with Spiller's agreement written on the back to visit Clemson in January 2006 should one day be placed in the football program's future museum. It will be remembered as one of the more significant items in Clemson's long and storied football history. "People always say in the recruiting process that you will know when you know," Spiller says. "You will know the perfect spot for you. I think honestly, when I first visited Clemson, I knew Clemson was the place for me."

I

THE MEETING IN THE BARRACKS

It is hard to imagine that college football turned 150 years old in 2019. It is even harder to imagine that Clemson's football program celebrated its 123rd birthday.

I'd like to tell you that there is a mind-blowing story about how Clemson first started playing the game that has inundated this sleepy little town on the foot of the Blue Ridge Mountains in western South Carolina. But the fact is, there really isn't one.

However, there is a story.

It began in 1896, three years after Clemson College first opened its doors. At the time, Clemson was a small agriculture and military school. In those days, the locals called it Clemson A&M. Many thought the "M" stood for "military," considering Clemson was a military college. However, the "A&M" stood for "Agriculture and Mechanical."

Clemson College was located in the small town of Calhoun, named in honor of John Ewing Calhoun, who had purchased a large area called Fort Hill in the late 1700s. Fort Hill Plantation remained in the family for nearly one hundred years until Calhoun's granddaughter Anna Maria and her husband, Ambassador Thomas Green Clemson, decided they wanted to transfer Fort Hill Plantation to the state of South Carolina following Clemson's death for the establishment of an agricultural college.

Little did anyone know that this was the inception of one of college football's most historic programs.

By the time Clemson opened its doors in 1893, college football was nearly a quarter century old and was being played just about everywhere in the South, including at schools such as Georgia, Auburn, South Carolina, Alabama and North Carolina. The game was sweeping through the country, and it did not take long for Clemson's cadets to want in.

"In 1896, Clemson College was quite a different-looking place to what it is now," wrote former Clemson president Walter Riggs, who also served as a professor and as its first football coach. "The campus was more or less covered with underbrush. There was no well-defined paths and very poor roads. There was only one barracks and only three other principal buildings—the Main Building, the Chemical Laboratory and Mechanical Hall.

"The Agricultural Laboratories and classrooms were in the main building. The post office was a little one-room wooden house to the right of the road as you pass Mechanical Hall, and about halfway between the road and the Calhoun Mansion. On the grass in front of this little post office, is where Clemson football had its beginning."

At the time, Riggs had sworn off athletics. He was ready to devote his time to his chosen profession of engineering, which is why he had left Alabama Polytechnic Institution—now known as Auburn—in 1895.

By this time, football's popularity was growing. North Carolina began its program in 1888, while South Carolina, Georgia and Alabama all began their programs in 1892. Furman, which is located in nearby Greenville, South Carolina, started its program in 1889.

Clemson, like all the others, started to get an itch for the game. When word got out that Clemson's newest engineering professor had played the game at Auburn, the cadets knew they had their in.

At Auburn, Riggs played catcher on the baseball team, where he was the captain. He also played left end on the football team and served as the team's manager as well. The cadets felt that if there was anyone who could help them start a football team, it was Professor Riggs. The question was, could they talk Riggs into it?

On September 30, 1896, thirty cadets met in the only barracks on campus to discuss starting a football team and to ask Riggs to help them get it off the ground. An organization known as the Clemson College Football Association was started, with Frank Tompkins elected as president, Charlie Gentry as secretary and treasurer, T.R. Vogel as manager and R.G. Hamilton as temporary captain. A committee of three people was appointed to consult Professor Riggs as to management of a football team and to ask for his aid as a coach.

Walter Riggs was Clemson's first head coach in 1896 and is responsible for bringing John Heisman to Clemson in 1900. *Clemson Athletic Communications.*

"When leaving Auburn, I had sworn off from athletics," Riggs wrote in the school newspaper. "But when the fall of 1896 came around and the Clemson boys wanted to get up a football team, the call of the wild was too strong, and again I found myself in a football suit, and the single-handed coach of the first Clemson football team."

The first practice began on October 5, 1896. It was held on a fifty-foot-wide, two-hundred-foot-long field in front of the college. It was not regulation size, but it was good enough to get things started. Ironically, Clemson now has arguably the best practice facility in the country. The Allen Reeves Football Complex encompasses nine acres, including three outdoor practice fields and the Poe Indoor Practice Facility.

But the game was still new to Clemson in 1896. Only one person at Clemson other than Riggs had seen a football at that time. That was Frank Tompkins, who played on the first team for Riggs. The players had to be

Clemson football players play one of their first games on Bowman Field in the early 1900s. *Clemson Athletic Communications.*

taught everything. They had never seen a football field or a football game and had no idea what to do or even how to stand or line up. "In looking back over a service of several years, I regard the introduction of intercollegiate football into Clemson College as one of the most valuable steps in the development of the institution," Riggs continued to write. "Long before its graduates could spread its fame as an institution of learning, its football teams had made the name of Clemson College known and respected throughout the nation."

Clemson traveled up the road to Greenville to play Furman in its first game, on October 31, 1896. Charlie Gentry scored the Tigers' first touchdown as they upset the Paladins, 14–6.

According to longtime Clemson associate sports information director Sam Blackman, a historian of Clemson athletics, Riggs was very demanding as a coach, and he set up a very strict training guideline for his players, one he expected to be followed accordingly. When the Tigers held their first practice, there were thirty players on the team. By the end of the last practice prior to the Furman game, there were just twenty-one.

Riggs also set up a training table and told his players they could not eat anything without first consulting with him or the team's trainer. He did not allow his players to drink anything with alcohol in it. They could not smoke or use any tobacco products, and lights had to be out by 11:00 p.m.

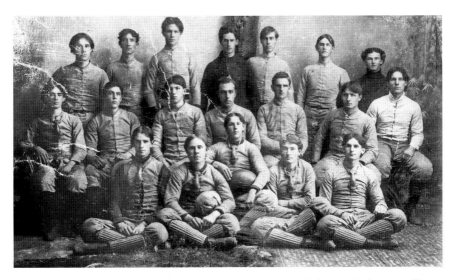

Clemson's first football team in 1896. The Tigers went 2-1 in their inaugural season. *Clemson Athletic Communications.*

Clemson finished its first season with a 2-1 record. It lost to South Carolina, 12–6, in the second game two weeks after the win over Furman. Nine days later, the Tigers defeated Wofford, 16–0. "When the season was over, Riggs told his players he wanted to devote more time as a professor, so he encouraged them to go out and find another coach," Blackman said.

Clemson went out and got W.M. Williams to coach its second team. The Tigers went 2-2 under Williams's guidance. In year three, they hired former Auburn assistant coach John Penton. He posted a 3-1 record, which included a 24–0 victory over South Carolina and a 23–0 win over Georgia Tech.

But Clemson could not afford to keep Penton for a second season, so Riggs agreed to coach the Tigers in 1899. Clemson went 4-2 in Riggs's second stint as head coach, including wins over South Carolina (34–0), North Carolina State (24–0) and Georgia Tech (23–0). "Though he did well as a football coach, the college needed Riggs elsewhere and he wanted that as well," Blackman said. "Riggs loved football and he wanted to see Clemson do well, but he had other responsibilities as a professor and as an administrator."

So, for the fifth straight year, Clemson was looking for a new football coach. This time was different, though. Clemson knew if it wanted to be serious about the game of football, it needed to find the funds and hire a coach, one who they could pay to stay for more than one season. This led to the creation of the Football Aid Society. Its first order of business was to find and fund a new football coach, one who would want to stay at Clemson for years to come. By its second meeting, the society had raised $372.50.

The Football Aid Society had the full support of Riggs, who aided in finding the Tigers' next head coach. Riggs had an idea of who that would be. He just had to go find him.

2

The Friendship between Riggs and Heisman

Without Walter Riggs there may not be a Heisman Trophy in college football.

In 1895, Riggs was charged with finding a new coach for Auburn's football program. Riggs, who had played and coached football at Auburn, learned about John Heisman through Carl Williams, who had played for Heisman when he was the coach at Oberlin a few years before.

Heisman had left coaching and moved to Marshall, Texas, where he worked as a tomato farmer. That's right, one of the greatest coaches in the history of college football was a tomato farmer. "After several weeks, I got into communication with Mr. Heisman, finding him in Texas engaged in raising tomatoes," Riggs wrote.

Tomato farming was not going too well for Heisman. He lost almost all of his capital in the farm. When Riggs found him in Texas and presented him the idea of getting back into coaching, Heisman jumped at the opportunity. Riggs offered Heisman $500 to become the new head coach at Auburn.

Though very well organized and tough, Heisman was not a particularly domineering figure. When he met his new football coach at the train depot in Auburn, Riggs thought he had made a mistake. Heisman was a small man, and his appearance did not impress the folks at Auburn at all. "I could not help but feel we had again made a mistake in the selection of a coach.… We made several before," Riggs wrote.

But Riggs and the others at Auburn soon realized they had the right guy for the job. Heisman was an innovator in football. He was always trying to find ways to advance the game and make it better. He introduced the center snap a year before Amos Alonzo Stagg introduced it at the University of Chicago. Heisman also introduced the lateral and eventually helped pioneer the forward pass.

Heisman was a master when it came to trickery, too. He invented the hidden ball trick, the handoff, the double lateral and the flea flicker. If he could find a loophole in the rules book, he would take advantage of it.

Bob Williams, who coached Clemson for six seasons between 1906 and 1915, once said Heisman rarely used the same trick play twice. "It did not acquire many days of practice to show that the Auburn team was in the hands of a master," Riggs explained.

In Heisman's first year at Auburn, those Tigers went 2-1, which included a 16–6 victory over Georgia and its great head coach, Pop Warner. Riggs left for Clemson that winter, and Heisman kept winning at Auburn. From 1895 to 1899, Heisman's Auburn teams posted a 12-4-1 record.

Though Auburn was doing well on the field, the program struggled financially. By the end of the 1897 season, the football team was $700 in debt, so Heisman took on a role as a theater producer, saving the program. While at Clemson, Riggs stayed in touch with Heisman. The two schools played against each other for the first time in 1899, as Heisman beat Riggs's Tigers, 34–0, at Auburn.

Already impressed with Heisman, Riggs was even more impressed by the way his team disposed of his own. Riggs knew it was time to take Clemson to a new level. Clemson finished the 1899 season 4-2 and in its four short years of existence produced an 11-6 record, including wins over South Carolina, Furman, Georgia Tech and North Carolina State. "By 1899, the Clemson football team had risen steadily until its talent was equal to that of any southern college, and the time had come to put on the long-planned finishing touch," Riggs wrote.

Riggs went to Birmingham, Alabama, to meet with Heisman. When he returned, he brought back a contract. Heisman would make $1,800 per year, a significant raise from what he was making at Auburn.

After four years of hoping to lure Heisman to Clemson, Riggs finally had the man he wanted to lead the Clemson football program. And he did not disappoint.

In his first season as head coach, Heisman led Clemson to its first undefeated season. The Tigers posted a 6-0 overall record, including a 3-0 mark in the Southern Independent Athletic Association (SIAA). At the end of the year, Clemson was crowned conference champions, the program's first championship.

John Heisman coached at Clemson from 1900 to 1903. He was 19-3-2 in his Clemson career. *Clemson Athletic Communications.*

During its championship season of 1900, Clemson posted four shutouts and outscored its opponents, 212–10.

Playing for Heisman was not easy. He expected his players to, first, be good students, and when they weren't being students, he wanted them to focus on football. He did not play any games. If a player was not serious about those two things, then Heisman would kick him off the team.

Heisman introduced new plays every week, and he expected his players to learn them fast. He did not tolerate players who could not learn the plays or his signals. "He was more concerned about a player being smart than so much brawn and strength," said Clemson athletic historian Sam Blackman. "He rather you'd be smart than big. He said, 'What good are you to have a large body but a small mind.' He wanted them to be smart because he did not have any patience for anyone who could not learn the plays or signals or things like that. He wanted you to be where you are supposed to be. He was very demanding. He was almost very eccentric. He wanted you to be well prepared. Dabo [Swinney] would really like him because of his preparation."

In his four seasons at Clemson, Heisman's teams posted a 19-3-2 record. His .833 winning percentage is still the best in Clemson history. His three losses came to Virginia Tech, South Carolina and North Carolina, and they were all by six points or less.

He racked up wins over Georgia, Alabama and Auburn. In all, Heisman led the Tigers to three SIAA championships in his four years at Clemson. "It is easy to say hiring Dabo was a great hire, but it is also equally as important that hiring Heisman helped put us on the map and helped build a foundation for football," Blackman said. "I think that raised the bar, if you will, and the standard. You know how Dabo is always talking about how best is the standard? Well, that standard, was set back then. They won all these football games…they beat Georgia, they beat Auburn, they beat Alabama. They tied Tennessee and won three conference championships which consisted of powerhouses like Vanderbilt and Suwannee, teams that used to be so good and we beat them. That set the standard."

To start the 1901 season, Clemson beat Guilford, 122–0. It is still the most points the Tigers have scored in a game, as well as the largest margin of victory. "They were winning big at halftime and Heisman told the team, 'Do not let up. They may have something up their sleeve.' They were winning like 100–0," Blackman chuckled.

The best story involving Heisman came in 1902, when Clemson traveled to Atlanta to play Georgia Tech. The Yellow Jackets' supporters were convinced they had the team that could knock off mighty Clemson. Heisman was a thinking man's kind of coach, though, so when word got back to him that Tech thought they could beat his team, Heisman decided to play a trick. In the days before Clemson was to play the Yellow Jackets, Heisman rounded up some cadets and shipped them off to Atlanta to impersonate the Clemson players.

When the fake Clemson team arrived in Atlanta the day before the game, Tech fans were surprised to see how scrawny the Tigers looked. Their appearance gave them nothing to be concerned about. It was the weakest team they had ever seen, causing some of the Yellow Jacket fans to laugh as the fake Clemson team got off the train.

If some fans still had concerns, those fears subsided when they saw the Clemson players leave their hotel rooms and hit the Atlanta night life. Tech fans even helped the Tigers enjoy themselves by buying them drinks and getting them dance partners.

Heisman asked his fake team to make a fuss and show out in Atlanta and to stay out all night if they wanted to. He wanted word to get back to Georgia Tech's team that Clemson's players were having a good time in Atlanta and were not focused on the football game.

They accomplished what Heisman was hoping for. Everyone had a great time, and word got back to Tech's campus and to its coaches and players. Meanwhile, the real Clemson team was staying a few miles north of Atlanta in Lula, Georgia, where they got plenty of rest for the game. Legend has it that some Tech fans who were partying with the fake Clemson players fell for the prank so well that they put money down on how their Yellow Jackets were going to beat the Tigers.

The next day, as Clemson jumped on top of the Yellow Jackets early, fans were amazed by how well the Tigers were playing despite a night of dancing and drinking. However, by halftime, they all figured out that they had been duked by Heisman.

Clemson rolled to an easy 44–5 victory. The trick was so good, the story made it on the Associated Press wire, becoming the first reported coast-to-coast story about Clemson football.

It was even worse for Tech the next year. Heisman did not need any tricks this time, as the Tigers went to Atlanta again and beat Georgia Tech, 73–0. Unfortunately for Clemson, Georgia Tech finally had enough. Its supporters and school officials were tired of being beat by Clemson and especially by Heisman.

After posting a 4-1-1 record at Clemson and tying Cumberland for another SIAA championship, Georgia Tech approached Heisman with an offer he could not refuse. They knew Heisman was a man about town. They found out about his theatrical background and knew that his wife was someone who loved the arts and the finer things in life, things she could not really get at Clemson.

"He got a big raise of $2,250. He also got promised 15 percent of the gate," Blackman said. "At that time, Atlanta had more spectators, so he did really well for himself. He also liked the social scene in Atlanta."

Heisman's first team tied Clemson, 11–11, in 1904, and then in 1905, they finally broke through and beat the Tigers for the first time, 17–10. After years of losing, Tech went 8-1-1 in Heisman's first season in Atlanta and 6-0-1 the next season. Clemson rallied to beat Tech and its former head coach in 1906 and 1907 while winning another SIAA title in the process in 1906.

However, Heisman won the last nine meetings against his old school and posted a 10-2-1 record against the Tigers during his sixteen seasons at Georgia Tech.

3

THE BIRTH OF IPTAY

In 1931, Jess Neely took over the Clemson football program. Neely had some big shoes to fill. The man he had replaced, Josh Cody, was the most successful coach at Clemson since John Heisman.

Cody turned the Tigers back into winners in the late 1920s, posting a 29-11-1 record in his four years as head coach (1927–30). Cody's departure came right at the start of the Great Depression, and Clemson, already a struggling agriculture college, did not have the means to keep up financially with its football program. The Depression had hit the program hard. It affected recruiting in Cody's last two seasons, while the money to keep up with facilities, equipment and supplies dropped off dramatically.

It was surprising that Neely wanted to come to Clemson at all. However, the Tennessee native, who was born in Smyrna, was known as a hard worker and as a guy who took on a challenge head-on. He knew the Clemson job was not going to be easy, but he believed he could turn the program back into the national power it had been under Heisman three decades earlier.

Neely came to Clemson from Alabama, where he had been an assistant coach under the great Wallace Wade. The Crimson Tide won the national championship in 1930 thanks to the help of a senior offensive lineman named Frank Howard. Neely thought the world of Howard, and when he accepted the Clemson job in 1931, he asked Howard to come along with him.

Prior to Clemson, Neely had been a winner wherever he played or coached. As a player, he was a part of two national championship teams at Vanderbilt and then helped the Crimson Tide win the 1930 championship.

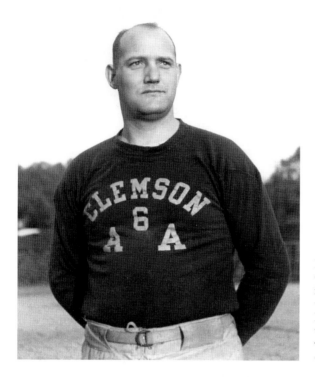

Frank Howard coached at Clemson for forty years, including thirty years as the head coach (1940–69). He is still the school's all-time leader in career wins with 165. *Clemson Athletic Communications.*

Neely's young staff consisted of Howard, Joe Davis and former Clemson standout Bob Jones. It is said the four men did everything to keep the athletic programs at Clemson running during the early years of Neely's tenure. From washing, repairing and sewing the uniforms; to maintaining the fields; to breaking down and moving makeshift bleachers from the gymnasium to the football field and to the baseball field, they did everything to save money.

The 1931 football season went about as well as the athletic department's budget would allow. Clemson won one game that year, a Week 3 victory over NC State. It was the first year in what came to be known as the "Seven Lean Years" at Clemson.

However, 1931 is one of the most important years in Clemson's athletic history. It was in this year that college athletics' first fundraising organization, otherwise known as a booster club, was conceived. And of all the places, it happened in a parking lot outside a football stadium in Florence, South Carolina.

On October 31, 1931, as they sat in a parked car outside old Florence Memorial Stadium following a 6–0 loss to the Citadel, Neely, Davis, Captain Frank Jervey and Captain Pete Heffner talked about the future of the football program. Jervey was working in Washington, D.C., at the time as a liaison between the military and the college. Heffner was a member of the military staff at Clemson and had a strong interest in athletics. He even assisted with coaching in his spare time.

Neely knew he was going to need something more if Clemson was going to stay competitive on the gridiron. Heffner suggested to Jervey that they ask the alumni for some money to help Neely finance the football program.

Jervey asked Neely how much they should ask for, and the football coach suggested a $50 Club. Neely felt if he could get $10,000 a year, he could build the kind of program that could compete for championships.

Through the help of Rupert H. Fike, the idea of fifty dollars a year was scaled down to ten dollars under the slogan "I Pay Ten A Year," best known as "IPTAY." As the powers that be tried to find a way to fund the football program, on the field, Neely slowly tried to put a winning team together. In 1932, the Tigers showed improvement but won just three games. They did the same in 1933. But Clemson's fortunes were about to change.

On August 21, 1934, Fike informed Neely the IPTAY Club had been organized and a constitution formulated. The constitution stated that the purpose of the Clemson Order of IPTAY "shall be to provide annual financial support to the athletic department at Clemson and to assist in every other way possible to regain for Clemson the high athletic standing which rightfully belongs to her."

Later that year, the Tigers finally beat rival South Carolina, 19–0, their first win over the Gamecocks under Neely. It began a seven-year win streak over Carolina, still longest by either team in the history of the rivalry. Clemson finished the 1934 season with a 5-4 record. The Tigers were once again winners at Clemson. However, this was just the beginning of where Neely would take the program.

While Neely was building his program at Clemson, IPTAY was growing. The club was to be a secret order: "Anyone who has matriculated at Clemson, has been employed by the college, or is a friend of the college, who can and will subscribe to the purpose of the order by taking the oath of secrecy and paying the initiation and yearly fees, when invited for membership, is eligible."

In the first year, attaining membership was tough. The Depression was still going on, so some members paid with post-dated checks; others gave two checks of $5.00 each, and others four at $2.50. Some payments were in the form of barter, as milk, sweet potatoes and turnip greens were used as acceptable payments.

Thanks to the help of Hoke Sloan and Red Richie, IPTAY started to prosper by its fourth year. The two men sold IPTAY; by 1942, membership climbed to about 1,900 and contributions exceed more than $21,000.

With IPTAY flourishing, the product on the field began to as well. In 1935, Clemson improved to 6-3 under Neely and again beat the hated Gamecocks, this time 44–0. The Tigers beat Carolina in 1936 and 1937, and though they did not have great years as a whole, they also did not have a losing record, setting the stage for one of the best four-year runs in Clemson history.

In 1938, Clemson produced a 7-1-1 team, which included a 34–12 win over the Gamecocks. In 1939, the Tigers pounded South Carolina, 27–0, on their way to an 8-1 record. At season's end, Clemson was extended an invitation to its first bowl game—the Cotton Bowl Classic—and of course accepted. The Tigers were scheduled to play the Eagles of Boston College on January 1, 1940, in Dallas, Texas.

Led by All-American Banks McFadden, Clemson finished No. 12 in the final Associated Press poll in 1939, marking the first time the program finished ranked in a national poll. The Eagles were ranked No. 11 and came into the game with a 9-1 record. Their only loss was to Cody's Florida team.

Following a Boston College field goal in the second quarter, Clemson got a 2-yard touchdown from Charlie Timmons, which gave the Tigers a 6–3 halftime lead. It turned out to be the final score. With the football program now playing and beating the best the country had to offer, enthusiasm for Clemson began to hit new highs, and IPTAY was there to reap the benefits. "When we came to Clemson in 1931, there wasn't twenty cents in the treasury; and when we left, there was over twenty thousand dollars," Neely said.

Neely left Clemson for Rice in 1940, and Howard succeed him. Things were good for Howard and IPTAY the first couple of years. In 1940, the Tigers followed the Cotton Bowl victory with its first Southern Conference Championship. In 1941, they went 7-2. Life was good. Clemson, once again, was a football power in the South. However, it did not last. By the end of 1941, America had gotten involved in War World II, and IPTAY began to flounder. Membership dropped to fewer than three hundred during the war; as a result, the football program suffered, too. From 1942 to 1944, Clemson endured three straight losing seasons. At times, because a lot of his players fought in the war, Howard barely had enough men to field a football team.

IPTAY did not stay down for long, and neither did Clemson football. They both survived the Second World War and, by the end of the decade, were both on top again. In 1948, Howard's Tigers, led by a freshman running back named Fred Cone, went 10-0 and finished No. 11 in the final AP

Jess Neely (*left*) and Frank Howard draw up a play. Howard coached under Neely from 1931 to 1939 before taking over as head coach after Neely left for Rice in 1940. *Clemson Athletic Communications.*

Poll. They were invited to the Gator Bowl in Jacksonville, Florida, after the season. They beat Missouri, 24–23.

Through the years, IPTAY has continued to find a way to be a leader in athletic fundraising. Its annual fund is one of the largest in the country, providing financial assistance for all of Clemson's seventeen sanctioned sports. Neely's dream of needing just $10,000 a year to run a championship program has turned into millions of dollars and has helped Clemson football become one of the nation's elite programs.

Through the 2019 season, Clemson has three national championships in football—1981, 2016 and 2018—and has won twenty-five conference championships, including a record nineteen in the Atlantic Coast Conference. Through the years, the Tigers have played in forty-six bowl games, winning twenty-five of them.

In his first twelve seasons, Dabo Swinney took the program to unprecedented heights, winning 130 games, two national championships and six ACC Championships. His teams have qualified for the College Football Playoff five straight years. "It is amazing to think about how far we've come over the last decade—how far we've come together," Swinney said in a letter to Clemson fans prior to the 2019 football season. "Our success is a direct result of strong leadership, unity and alignment in all areas. Our Board of Trustees, led by Chairman Smyth McKissick, President Clements, Director of Athletics Dan Radakovich and Deputy Director of Athletics Graham Neff are the best in the business. Their partnership and friendship mean a lot to me. Our program does not rise to the championship level we've achieved without their unwavering support and dedication. I am so grateful for their continued faith and belief in me."

In 2019, Clemson spent more than $2.7 million on football scholarships. The money covers the players' tuition, room and board, books, three meals a day, fees and transportation for school. That's not all. The players now train in one of the more luxurious training facilities in the country at the Allen Reeves Football Complex, a $55 million facility that opened in January 2017. Inside the 142,500-square-foot facility is a 25,000-square-foot weight room, a state-of-the-art training facility, a wellness area, a nap room, a barbershop, a golf simulator, a bowling alley, an outdoor basketball court, a miniature-golf course, a sand volleyball court and a wiffleball field.

There is also the Poe Indoor Practice Facility, which was built in 2012. It allows the team to practice and train indoors when weather conditions get too stringent outside. Then, of course, there is Memorial Stadium, which seats 81,500 fans and is considered one of the best football atmospheres in the country.

It does not end there. The players also eat at PAW Diner, where their meals are supervised by a full-time sports nutritionist and are prepared by a full-time chef. On the academic side of things, the players have academic advisors and tutors to help them graduate. PAW Journey, a program run by former All-American linebacker Jeff Davis, allows players to experience things outside of football such as internships, mission trips and much more.

In 2018, IPTAY raised $38.2 million in its annual fund; $15.1 million in major gifts, including cash, real estate and securities; $5.1 million in planned gifts and endowments; and $6.6 million in premium seating and suites in Memorial Stadium, basketball's Littlejohn Coliseum and baseball's Doug Kingsmore Stadium.

IPTAY even has a new home, located next to the West End Zone in Memorial Stadium. The twenty-nine-thousand-square-foot structure, which also houses the Clemson Athletic Department Ticket Office, cost $10 million to build and was funded by donors and private gifts. The new facility opened in the spring of 2020.

4

MEMORIAL STADIUM

College Football's Real Death Valley

When Jesse Neely left Clemson for Rice in 1940, he left the job to Frank Howard, who accompanied him to Clemson from Alabama in 1931. Neely thought a lot of Howard, and he wanted to see him succeed as a head coach. However, Neely gave Howard one piece of advice before heading to Houston. "Don't ever let them talk you into building a big stadium," Neely said to Howard. "Put about ten thousand seats behind the YMCA. That's all you'll ever need."

As we all know, Howard did not listen to Neely's advice. Soon after Neely left, Howard began drawing up plans for a twenty-thousand-seat stadium located in a natural valley a little west of Historic Riggs Field, now the soccer stadium at Clemson. By the end of the 1940 season, trees were already being cleared in the valley, and Howard was right there cutting them down and clearing the path.

According to legend, when the concrete was later poured, Howard—known for chewing his tobacco—placed a bite of chew in each corner of the stadium, permanently leaving a part of him in the stadium.

The seeding of the grass was the biggest issue. They had about forty people helping lay the sod. About three weeks into the project, they had gotten just about halfway through. "I told them it had taken us three weeks to get that far and I would give them three more weeks' pay for however long it took to finish," Howard said. "I also told them we would have 50 gallons of ice cream when we got through. After that, it took them about three days to do the rest of the field. Then we sat down in the middle of the field and ate up that whole 50 gallons."

Memorial Stadium, named in honor of the former Clemson students and alumni who had sacrificed their lives in the two world wars, opened its gates for the first time on September 19, 1942. "The gates were hung at 1:00 p.m., and we played at 2:00 p.m.," Howard later said.

Clemson beat Presbyterian, 32–13, in front of an estimated crowd of five thousand fans in that first game. "The way I see it, Memorial Stadium is Coach Howard. He designed it. He cut down the trees. He poured the concrete and he laid down the grass. He about did it all," said former head coach Danny Ford.

Though Howard built Memorial Stadium, he is not the person responsible for its nickname. And, just in case an LSU fan is reading this book, Tiger Stadium in Baton Rouge, Louisiana, is not college football's real Death Valley. That distinction belongs to Clemson.

Cally Gault remembered his first trip to Clemson quite well. A freshman at Presbyterian at the time, he and his Blue Hose teammates came to Memorial Stadium and were thrashed, 76–0. The Tigers netted 516 yards on the ground as fourteen different players carried the ball on September 22, 1945. Clemson freshman Bobby Gage, who went on to play for the Pittsburgh Steelers, led the Tigers with 144 yards, including an 88-yard touchdown run. All eleven of Clemson's touchdowns came on the ground that afternoon, which is a record that still stands today.

Soon after being beat so bad by the Tigers, Presbyterian head coach Lonnie McMillian gave Memorial Stadium its iconic nickname. "After we were beaten so badly in 1945, Coach McMillian and us players referred to the Clemson trip as going 'to Death Valley,'" said Gault. "I'm not sure when the press picked up on it, but I'm sure it was real soon."

The press picked up on it because McMillian would tell them, "I'm taking my boys to Death Valley," when he spoke about the Clemson trip. Presbyterian and Clemson opened the season every year from 1930 to 1957.

Gault was a player and coach during most of those years, and none of the PC teams he was on came close to beating Clemson, which became relevant on the national scene in the late 1930s and early 1940s. "I was 16 years old as a freshman when I came to PC, and playing in Death Valley was special," said Gault, who was also the head coach at Presbyterian from 1962 to 1984. "I do remember this more than anything—it was hot, and I mean real hot at Clemson. You haven't felt hot until you played in Death Valley in early September."

Howard soon picked up on the moniker "Death Valley" and started referring to Memorial Stadium as such when he went to IPTAY meetings or when speaking to the press. The earliest accounts of Howard using the nickname came in the late 1940s and early '50s, when the Tigers were making regular trips to bowl games like the Gator Bowl, the Orange Bowl and the Sugar Bowl.

In 1957, a young athlete by the name of Billy Cannon made his way to LSU. A local kid from Baton Rouge, Cannon was one of the more sought-after players in the country. He scored 39 touchdowns his senior year of high school, allowing him to earn All-American honors. Cannon was also a track star, clocked running 100 yards in 9.4 seconds and 40 yards in 4.12 seconds.

At LSU, Cannon lived up to the hype. As a three-year starter in 1957, '58 and '59, he set all sorts of records while leading the Tigers to their first national championship in 1958 and winning the Heisman Trophy in 1959.

But his most memorable moment and the one that started the controversy about which stadium owns the right to be called the original "Death Valley" came on Halloween night in 1959. Trailing No. 3 Ole Miss, 3–0, late in the game, Cannon had his Heisman moment when he took a punt at his own 11-yard line, broke seven tackles before he got to his own 40, then ran away from everyone the final 60 yards for the game-winning score.

In Marty Mule's 1993 book *Eye of the Tiger: One Hundred Years of LSU Football*, he describes that night and at the same time speaks to the origin of how Tiger Field became known as "Death Valley." In the chapter called "Death Valley USA," on page 123, Mule writes about the reaction to Cannon's 89-yard punt return to beat Ole Miss. "The noise level generated by Cannon's run is to have supposed to have brought people scurrying from their homes for miles around to see what happened, part of why Tiger Field was dubbed 'Deaf Valley.' The name 'Death Valley'—which was used first at Clemson—was picked when the original term was not properly enunciated, and misunderstood."

In other words, LSU never intended Tiger Field to be called "Death Valley." The locals could not say "Deaf Valley" correctly. Also, it proves that Tiger Field's nickname did not come until many years after Clemson began using the moniker, and Mule acknowledges Clemson used it first.

Former LSU and South Carolina head coach Paul Dietzel confirmed Mule's writings. Dietzel coached the Tigers from 1955 to '61, and he said the nickname "Death Valley" was not used for Tiger Field while he was the head coach in Baton Rouge. "I don't think so. That came a little later," said Dietzel in a 2012 interview with *The Clemson Insider*.

Through the years, Death Valley has lived up to its nickname. Prior to the 2020 season, the Tigers totaled 316 wins in seventy-eight years and have won 75 percent of their games (316-102-7). Under Dabo Swinney, Death Valley has never been so good. Heading into 2020, the Tigers are 71-6 under Swinney, including a 60-3 home record from 2011 to 2019. Clemson had a 21-game home winning streak from 2013 to 2016 and entered the 2020 season with a record 22-game home winning streak.

The Tigers are 47-2 at Death Valley from 2013 through the beginning of the 2019 season. "It is one of the best places to play in college football," said Jimbo Fisher, who coached against Clemson during his time at Florida State and now at Texas A&M. "It is Death Valley. It will be loud."

Through the years, Memorial Stadium has grown and changed its appearance. In 1958, 18,000 seats were added, and in 1960, 5,658 seats were built in the west end zone as a response to an increase in ticket demands.

With the west end zone stands, capacity increased to fifty-three thousand. It stayed that way until 1978, when Clemson added an upper deck on the south side of the stadium. In 1983, an upper deck was added on the north side, swelling the capacity to more than eighty thousand.

Over the years, Memorial Stadium has packed in more than eighty-six thousand diehard Clemson fans. "There will be a lot of orange. If you like orange, there will be a lot of that," said Fisher, whose teams are 1-4 at

Since 2013, Clemson has posted a 47-2 record at Memorial Stadium. The Tigers went into the 2020 season with a 22-game home winning streak. The Clemson Insider.

Death Valley. "There will be a lot of happy fans. They are a great fan base. Tremendous fan base, a classy fan base. But very loud and hard to go play in. Like in [the SEC], it is like the venues you are going to play in, in our league. It is eighty thousand something or ninety thousand or whatever it is. They love their ball and they are passionate about it, that is for sure."

Today, Memorial Stadium is one of the largest on-campus stadiums in the country, with crowds that swell to more than eighty-one thousand. "We go to a lot of great venues for college football, but this doesn't take a back seat to any place. In terms of the atmosphere, stadium, noise and facilities, this is a special place on a Saturday night," ESPN analyst Todd Blackledge said.

5

FRANK HOWARD

Clemson's Best-Known Ambassador

W hen you think of where Clemson football is today, it is hard to imagine where it came from. There was a time when a good portion of the country had no idea where Clemson was located. Clemson was once a small agriculture and military college located at the base of the Blue Ridge Mountains in western South Carolina. It is still a small town today, as close to fourteen thousand residents reside there when school is not in session.

It's hard to imagine when driving through downtown—which, by the way, has just three traffic lights on College Avenue—that this small city houses one of the best college football programs in the country. However, that was not always the case.

When Jesse Neely became head coach at Clemson in 1931, he brought with him a young and energetic man who was just removed from his days as a football player at the University of Alabama. In 1930, Frank Howard helped Wallace Wade's Alabama team win a national championship. The Crimson Tide had just whipped Washington State, 24–0, in the 1931 Rose Bowl when he accompanied Neely to Clemson.

Howard was offered a high school coaching position in Hopkinsville, Kentucky, before he received a letter from Neely offering him a job at Clemson. Though the high school position was $200 more than what Neely had offered, Howard decided to join Neely in Clemson without hesitation. "In 1931, you didn't ask much about a job," Howard was quoted in the 1983 book *The Clemson Tigers: From 1896 to Glory.* "You took anything that was available. You were lucky to have any job. Going to Clemson was the best decision I ever made."

Nine months later, Neely laid down the foundation of the country's first booster club organization when he and three other men came up with the idea of IPTAY. By the end of the decade, IPTAY had helped Clemson climb the mountain of respectability when it accepted an invitation to play in the 1940 Cotton Bowl Classic in Dallas.

With an 8-1 record and a No. 12 national ranking, the Tigers were going to play Frank Leahy's Boston College team, which went 9-1 in 1939. The Eagles were ranked No. 11 in the final Associated Press Poll and were considered the odds-on favorite to beat this upstart college from the South that was making its first bowl appearance.

However, no one in Boston knew where Clemson was, so the *Boston Post* assigned one of its writers, Gerry Hern, to find out just exactly where Clemson was located and what it was like. In 1939, the city of Clemson was not known as Clemson; instead, it was known as Calhoun, named after former vice president of the United States John C. Calhoun.

Calhoun's daughter Anna Maria owned the land that Clemson University sits on today. Back then, of course, it was known as the Fort Hill estate, located just outside the city of Pendleton. When she died in 1875, Anna Marie willed her land to her husband, Thomas Green Clemson, who also outlived his four children. In the mid-1880s, Clemson drafted a final will, leaving the land to the state of South Carolina to be used for the establishment of a land-grant college, the Clemson Agricultural College of South Carolina.

Clemson died at the age of eighty in 1888. The military college was founded a year later and, by 1893, had opened its doors to 446 cadets. The city of Calhoun was later renamed Clemson in 1943, in large part because its character was designed around the college.

When Hern finally made it to Clemson in December 1939, he was amazed at what he found. Clemson was smaller than he expected. In fact, he documented how he was almost run over by a mule when he first got to town. One of the mules had gotten out of Mayor Frank Clinkscales's stable, which was located in the middle of town.

Hern spent a week in Clemson and was quite fascinated with it and the people who lived there. The people were very friendly, and the small-town atmosphere the Clemson players and coaches experienced every day was different than what the players and coaches experienced in the big city of Boston.

While Hern was discovering Clemson, Neely was supposedly having talks with the people at Rice University to fill its head-coaching vacancy. Though flattered, Neely was focused more on the Cotton Bowl and how he was going to beat Boston College.

Of course, in a small town such as Clemson, it does not take long for rumors to spread. Word got out that Neely was leaving Clemson. When the team made its way to Dallas to play in the Cotton Bowl, the rumors picked up. As accounted in the 2017 book *Clemson: Where the Tigers Play*, Neely supposedly told a small group of men in his hotel room prior to the Cotton Bowl, including Howard, that he was going to take the job at Rice. Despite the rumors, the Tigers went on to beat Boston College, 6–3. Charlie Timmons, who rushed for 115 yards in the game, scored what turned out to be the winning touchdown on a 2-yard run in the second quarter.

Reports surfaced after the game that Neely had accepted a five-year contract to become Rice's new head coach. Neely would not comment on the reports, but a few weeks later, he indeed left Clemson for Rice.

While Neely was leaving Clemson, Howard came to love it. In 1933, he married a local girl, Anna Tribble, of nearby Anderson, South Carolina. Clemson became his home, and he had no desire to leave.

After Neely left Clemson for Rice, the athletic council got together to find a successor. Howard, who was waiting in the back of the room to be interviewed as a possible candidate, was nominated by Professor Sam Rhodes as the head coach.

As the legend goes, once Rhodes made his nomination, Howard seconded the nomination. The council then got together and voted Howard as Clemson's seventeenth head football coach. He received a four-year deal, which he later admitted he misplaced several years later on a business trip. It was the only contract he signed in his thirty years as the Tigers' head coach. After his first four years ran out, he formalized a yearly deal to stay on as head coach with a handshake. "They never asked for another contract and they never offered me one," Howard said. "I guess I am the only coach whoever wore out three college presidents."

Howard may have worn out three school presidents, but he did not wear out his welcome at Clemson. It is said that Howard did more for Clemson than any other football coach, putting the school on the national map.

Off the field, Howard was charming and appealing, using his rich southern draw to appeal to the boosters and the media. On the field, he was a strict disciplinarian who demanded a lot from his players. He was the perfect match to be the face of Clemson's football program. "When you

Clemson's Frank Howard. *Clemson Athletic Communications*.

think of Clemson football, you think of Coach Howard," former Clemson coach Danny Ford said. "He is the one who set it up for us and what we were able to accomplish during our time here. People knew about Clemson long before us because of Coach Howard."

Howard spent thirty years walking up and down the sideline of the stadium he built. His Clemson teams won a combined 165 games, just one of three active coaches at the time of his retirement with 150 or more victories. His first team at Clemson went 6-2-1 and won the Southern Conference, the program's first conference championship since 1906. In all, Howard won eight conference championships, including six Atlantic Coast Conference Championships. He also guided the program to national prominence with multiple bowl appearances in prestigious games like the Orange Bowl, Sugar Bowl and Gator Bowl.

His 1948 team went undefeated and untied with an 11-0 record, which it capped with a win over Missouri in the 1949 Gator Bowl. In 1951, the Tigers completed another undefeated season, 9-0-1, with a win over Miami in the 1951 Orange Bowl Classic.

It was the 1951 Orange Bowl that made it Howard's mission to publicize Clemson as often as he could. Following the regular season, the No. 10 Tigers accepted an invitation to play in its first Orange Bowl game. Clemson had rolled through the 1950 season, winning seven of its eight regular-season games by 21 or more points and six of those by 27 or more points. The lone blemish was a 14–14 tie to archrival South Carolina on Big Thursday in Columbia.

Many believed the Tigers had the best single-wing attack in the country, led by halfback Fred Cone, whom Howard called the greatest player he ever coached. However, no one in South Florida was happy when it was announced that Clemson would play undefeated and 15th-ranked Miami in the Orange Bowl. They wanted to know why their local team and prestigious bowl game was hosting what they felt was a school no one knew anything about.

When Howard got word of this reaction, he was not happy. It bothered him. Normally, he would just brush off something of this matter. However, this one got to him. He felt his team and Clemson deserved more respect. During a banquet at the end of the regular season, Howard vented his displeasure. "Shucks, we've won the only two bowl games we've been in, which don't seem to mean much to some folks," he said. "They ought to read the AP poll if they want to know about Clemson."

In the end, Howard and the Tigers got their respect with a 15–14 victory over the Hurricanes. Ironically, it was an unheralded, nonscholarship defensive guard named Sterling Smith who broke through the line from the Miami 1-yard line and tackled a Hurricane running back in the end zone for a safety, winning the game for the Tigers.

The win over Miami put Clemson on the map, and the Tigers' head coach wanted to make sure they stayed there. However, though Clemson had played in another Orange Bowl, losing to Colorado in the 1958 Orange Bowl Classic, they felt disrespected again after it was announced that national champion LSU was going to play the Tigers in the 1959 Sugar Bowl Classic in New Orleans.

Clemson had won at least seven games four straight years—it was a ten-game regular season back in those days—and were 8-2 and finished 12th in the final AP Poll in 1958. Sugar Bowl officials were impressed by the ACC champions and extended the team an invitation to play in their bowl game.

The local press wanted to know why the Sugar Bowl picked such a lowly school such as Clemson to play the mighty Bayou Tigers from Baton Rouge. The New Orleans *Times-Picayune* wrote, "Oh, Frank Howard, we beg of you to warn that team of yours that LSU now reigns supreme; and when it reigns, it pours."

However, Howard wasn't to be outdone. He later got the best of the media, and the "good ole boys" down in Baton Rouge were impressed.

Frank Howard called Fred Cone the best player he ever coached. Cone helped Clemson to an 11-0 record in 1948. *Clemson Athletic Communications.*

"This coaching business will get you if you let it. More letters come in from alumni and even small boys and girls telling me what I have to do about [Billy] Cannon and the Chinese Bandits," Howard said in a speech to the Biloxi, Mississippi chamber of commerce prior to the Sugar Bowl while waving newspaper clippings from local scribes. "If I didn't have a coaching job, I'd be between the shafts of a plow. But with all its trials, coaching beats plowing. I've always found you meet a lot of dumb guys in the newspaper and radio business, and tonight's no exception."

It wasn't just Howard and the Tigers flying the Clemson flag that week. In New Orleans, a local sportswriter marveled at the amount of orange seen in the city in the days leading up to the game. The week before, it was reported that LSU had asked for more tickets for the game, thinking Clemson had returned a lot because the school was small. LSU officials were stunned to find out Clemson sold out its allotment of tickets and had also asked for extras.

Clemson orange was all over Bourbon Street and the French Quarter. One writer reported that it was a sea of orange and that everyone knew where it was coming from, with so many cars with South Carolina tags driving up and down Bourbon Street.

The ACC's Tigers held their own against the national champions in the Sugar Bowl. Cannon's 9-yard touchdown pass on a halfback option to Mickey Mangham in the third quarter turned out to be the only score in a 7–0 LSU victory. "Clemson is the best football team we met this year," Cannon said after the game. "They really hit."

With Howard boasting about Clemson to the media and then with his teams' performing well on the biggest of stages, no one was asking anymore "Where is Clemson?" or "Why are we playing them?"

Clemson went on to win another ACC Championship the following year while posting an 8-2 mark and a No. 11 ranking in the final AP Poll. However, none of the bowls extended an invitation to the Tigers, who were getting nervous, especially with schools like Georgia going to the Orange Bowl and Georgia Tech being invited to the Gator Bowl. There were two bowls left with open invitations: the Liberty Bowl in Philadelphia and the new Bluebonnet Bowl in Houston.

Clemson was eventually invited to play No. 7 TCU in the Bluebonnet Bowl. "This year there were no special gimmicks. The New Orleans newspapers had been pretty critical of us last year before the Sugar Bowl, but you know something? We might show some of those other bowls. It looks like we will have a great crowd," Howard said.

Frank Howard (*right*) and Sterling Smith were carried off the field following Clemson's 15–14 win over Miami in the 1951 Orange Bowl Classic. *Clemson Athletic Communications.*

The Tigers went on to show those other bowls something, all right. Trailing 7–3 entering the fourth quarter, Clemson scored 20 unanswered points in the fourth quarter for a 23–7 victory over the Horned Frogs. The Tigers' 23 points were the most points scored against TCU in fifty-six games.

Howard won three more ACC Championships in the 1960s before hanging up his whistle after the 1969 season due to boosters and fans who thought it was time for a change. "It was not what I wanted personally, but what I think is best for Clemson," he told a packed press conference on December 10, 1969.

Some in the media who covered Howard for years did not agree with how Clemson handled the change, but they applauded the way in which Howard handled it. The *Charlotte Observer*'s Herman Helms wrote, "The haunting question now is this: Has football become so cruelly competitive that a contributor such as Frank Howard cannot pick his own time to go?

"No time would be the right time for an original, a one and only kind of man like Frank Howard, to go. But it was inevitable that it would happen in some season soon.

"He was 60 years old and he had coached for 39 years. No time would be the right time, but it would have been nice if he could have picked the time, if he could have given the last signal that closed a great career.

"But it didn't happen that way. He left without rancor, without bitterness. A man who has given 39 years of his life to a cause isn't about to hurt the cause. Frank Howard would not dare hurt Clemson.

"He tried to make it look right, for Clemson's sake, but he did not succeed. The timing was the giveaway. No coach plans to quit three days before signing day for high school recruits. No coach plans to quit at a time like that and particularly if his successor is not at his side. The timing told the story, an unpleasant story.

"And old warrior left because things had become unpleasant for him. And old warrior left trying to look brave in the face but with tears in his heart. A contributor who gave so much to a game and a school and a state left because people have short memories.

"That's the way it was. It was sad. There is no other way to say it."

Howard stayed on as Clemson's athletic director until he officially retired from athletics in 1974. He never held a grudge for being pushed out earlier than he wanted to go. Howard loved Clemson too much to do that. He was still talking up the program to anyone who would listen. He always joked that he had to leave Clemson as its football coach because of health reasons. "The alumni got sick of me," he would say.

Even in retirement, Howard continued as Clemson's biggest ambassador, and because of his quick wit and sense of humor, he became a popular guest speaker all over the country. The media, especially columnists, would call him just to hear one of his stories.

Almost until his death in January 1996, Howard booked speaking engagements and, in doing so, sold Clemson's brand and made sure everyone knew about Clemson. From the day he took over for Jess Neely in 1940, Howard's one mission was to make sure everyone knew where Clemson, South Carolina, was.

Former Clemson spokesman Sam Blackman documented it best in Clemson football's *Media Guide Supplement* when he wrote, "When Howard died at the age of 86 it forever silenced a voice that had been synonymous with Clemson for nearly 65 years. He was the school's best-known ambassador."

6

HOWARD'S ROCK

"The Most Exciting 25 Seconds in College Football"

Football is a way of life in Clemson, South Carolina.
Clemson has played America's favorite sport for all but three years since it opened its doors in 1893. Through the years, Clemson traditionally has been one of college football's most consistent teams, with three national championships, twenty-five conference titles and forty-six bowl appearances.

The stories, legendary coaches and traditions at Clemson make up some the of the best in the sport. No tradition or story is better at Clemson than the tradition of Howard's Rock, especially with how it started.

When Memorial Stadium opened its doors in 1942, the football team's dressing room was located at old Fike Fieldhouse, down the street on Williamson Road on the east side of the stadium. The Tigers would dress at Fike and then take the short walk down Williamson Road to the stadium.

From the first day the gates opened to Memorial Stadium, prior to warmups, Howard had his team enter through the east-side gate, where they would run down the hill instead of walking around. It was a tradition that was born for the most part out of convenience.

At first, there was no carpet for the players to run down. There was no band playing "Tiger Rag." There were no fans. It was just the team running down the hill to do warmups. It was not really that special at all. "When I first started coming to Clemson games in 1964, they did not run down the hill like they do now," former Clemson senior associate sports information director Sam Blackman said. "When Coach Howard was here, they dressed inside old Fike Fieldhouse and would leave to go to the stadium from there. They would walk down Williamson Road. I can still see those helmets bouncing up and down now as they were coming down the street. You could see the tip of the orange helmets just over the fence.

"Coach Howard had them enter the stadium through a fence that they used to sit at the top of the hill, and they would come down the hill and into the stadium. They did it as convenience more than anything else."

However, eventually, fans started showing up a little bit earlier for each home game and would cheer the Tigers on as they came down the hill. Over the years, the crowds grew from a few people to a few hundred. "My father and I always went to watch that. There wasn't much fan fair then as there is now. Maybe a couple hundred people, if that many," Blackman explained. "But, keep in mind, they came down the hill in those days prior to warmups. A lot of the fans were still tailgating at that time and had yet to enter the stadium."

In the late 1950s, Clemson alum S.C. Jones was driving through Death Valley, California, when he stopped his car and picked up a ten-pound rock and put it in his trunk. He carried the rock all the way back to Clemson, where Memorial Stadium had taken on the moniker "Death Valley." Jones thought it would be nice for Clemson's Death Valley to have a rock from the real Death Valley in California. Howard accepted the gift and placed it in his office, where it sat on the floor for nearly seven years.

Legend has it that Howard used the rock as a doorstop and, when he began to clean his office one day in the spring of 1966, he decided he did not want it anymore. The longtime Clemson coach told Gene Willimon, the executive secretary of IPTAY at the time, to get rid of the rock. He suggested to Willimon to toss it over in the Valley with the rest of the rocks around the stadium. Willimon did not think that was such a nice thing to do, since Jones had gone out of his way to bring Howard this rock from Death Valley, California. So, without telling Howard, he placed the rock at the top of the east hill on a pedestal under the scoreboard.

It was in place in time for the opening game of the 1966 season as the Tigers hosted Virginia. The Cavaliers went up 18 points, 28–10, on the Tigers by the end of the third quarter and looked as if they would get their first win over a Clemson football team. But the Tigers rallied for one of the greatest comebacks in Death Valley history and won the game, 40–35. Clemson went on to an undefeated season that year at Memorial Stadium, giving birth to Howard's tale of how his rock has "mystical powers." Howard figured he could use this tale to his advantage, maybe giving his players a little extra motivation.

Frank Howard poses with his famous rock prior to the 1989 football season. *Clemson Athletic Communications.*

At dinner the Friday night before the Tigers' season-opener against Wake Forest in 1967, Howard told his team, 'Here, boys. If any of you boys are gonna go out and give me 120 percent, I'll let you rub my rock; and it'll give you supernatural powers,'" Howard is quoted in the book *The Clemson Tigers: From 1896 to Glory.* His players promised they would. The next day, they rubbed Howard's Rock, ran down the hill and beat Wake Forest, 23–6. The Legend of Howard's Rock was born.

Clemson players have since touched Howard's Rock and run down the hill more than four hundred times. These days, thanks to former head coach Red Parker's creativeness prior to the Texas A&M game in 1973, Clemson leaves the locker room about ten minutes before kickoff under the WestZone of Memorial Stadium and boards a group of buses that carries them to the top of the east side of the stadium, where they charge down the hill and into Death Valley.

After Howard retired in 1969, Hootie Ingram was hired as the new coach for the 1970 season. As part of changing its image and upgrading its facilities, Clemson built a brand-new locker room, located under the stands in the west end zone.

Because of the new locker room, Ingram made a logical decision that the team would run on to the field from the dressing room, instead of running down the hill. From the start of the 1970 season until the next-to-last home game of the 1972 season, the Tigers did not run down the hill.

However, in hopes of creating some solidarity prior to the 1972 season finale against rival South Carolina, defensive back Ben Anderson, who went on to become a lawyer and served as general counsel and secretary to the board of trustees at Clemson for twenty-one years, led a group of seniors to Ingram's office the week of the game. One of those seniors was future Furman and Vanderbilt head coach Bobby Johnson. "I went along to the meeting as support, but this was all Ben's idea," Johnson said following Anderson's death in 2015. "He had it all planned out. It was like he was trying his first law case."

Ingram liked Anderson's proposal and even assisted with the plan on how they were going to use buses to get the players from the west side of the stadium to the east side. Anderson's plan worked out perfectly, and the Tigers beat the Gamecocks, 7–6, in a rainy afternoon at Death Valley.

Ingram was let go as Clemson's head coach following the win over South Carolina. Parker was named the new head coach in 1973. When his first Clemson team ran out of the dressing room for the first time on September 8, 1973, against the Citadel, Red Parker remembered that the atmosphere was pretty stale that afternoon. In fact, as he recalled, there was no energy at all in the stadium. And, because of that, he said the Tigers played stale, squeaking out a 14–12 victory.

"When I went to Clemson, attendance was way down," Parker said. "It was just a period of time when the enthusiasm was not the way it is now. It was kind of a difficult time out on that football field before the game and during the game.

"It was not something that was fun."

That following Monday morning, Parker went to athletic director Bill McLellan and told him they needed to do something to get the enthusiasm back in Death Valley. "I thought about a lot of things I had heard about Clemson before I went there," Parker said. "One of the things that struck me as being a goldmine of potential was the Tigers running down the hill in the east end zone. I saw that as a spirit lifter.

"Coach Howard had done it for years, and I felt like it did all that he wanted it to do. He accomplished a great deal with that, and keep in mind running down the hill was Coach Howard's deal."

Parker was stunned when he learned that Clemson stopped running down the hill. It disappointed him, because he knew that it was one of the things that made Clemson special and unique to all the other schools. "Well, at that point right there, after the first home game, I went to Bill McLellan, and I said, 'Bill, there is not enough spirit and enough energy and enthusiasm in the stadium. There is just not enough to have what you have to have to play major college football. That is just the way it is.'

"He said, 'What do you want to do?' And I said, 'I want to run down the hill.' Bill at that point said, 'We can't run down the hill because the reason we quit is because we spent thousands and thousands of dollars on a new dressing room on the [west] end of the stadium.' Which was true, they did. They did spend a lot of money on those dressing rooms, which they had to have. It was an absolute must. They had to have those dressing rooms down there, so I went back to my office and I got to thinking."

During that period of thought, "The most exciting 25 seconds in college football" was reintroduced to Tiger fans. However, it wasn't done the way they remembered it.

Learning how Howard's teams ran down the hill, and why they did it, helped Parker get creative. Knowing he had to use the west end zone locker rooms, Parker thought of a plan that has been used by every Clemson coach since. What Parker created is what he called one of the most motivating events in sports, and one of the best recruiting tools in college football.

Clemson's next home game in 1973 did not occur until October 6. The Tigers were coming off back-to-back road losses to Georgia and Georgia Tech, and Parker was anxious to see how the crowd would respond as Clemson ran down the hill prior to its battle with Texas A&M.

"I don't mind thinking farfetched at times, so I decided at that point it would be worthwhile for me to figure out a way to run down the hill because you always have a little bit of dead time before the game," he said. "I thought it would be a worthwhile opportunity to seize this and move on with it. We always used two busses to go to the motel where we stayed for the pre-game meal, and then we bussed into the stadium and dressed for the game. Well, after we got on the field and warmed up, we came back in the dressing room and did everything we needed to do.

"At that point, instead of going out onto the field for the game, we had the players get on the buses. We then drove them around the stadium to the other end of the field, got them off the buses and came down the hill together. That made a big difference in our stadium. It got people excited."

It still does today. Nobody in college football has such a unique entrance as does Clemson. "In my opinion, running down the hill is one of the greatest motivators in all of college football," Parker said. "In fact, when I was at Clemson, we believed if we could get the prospects there on a Saturday afternoon when the Tigers ran down the hill, we had a chance to recruit them. And we brought in a lot of them."

Since that October afternoon in 1973, the Tigers have boarded the buses on the west side of the stadium and drove around to the east side, where they have unloaded, rubbed Howard's Rock and charged down the hill and into the Valley below.

Charlie Pell and the Tigers get ready to run down the hill prior to a game in 1978. Pell was 18-4-1 in his two seasons at Clemson. *Clemson Athletic Communications.*

Dabo Swinney comes racing down the hill for the first time prior to the 2008 Georgia Tech game at Death Valley. *Clemson Athletic Communications.*

In 1985, the Friday before the Georgia game, CBS announcer Brent Musburger told Hall of Fame Clemson sports information director Bob Bradley that the Tigers' charging down the hill and into Death Valley was "The Most Exciting 25 Seconds in College Football."

Years later, prior to the start of another Clemson-Georgia game at Death Valley in 2013, Musburger added on the ABC broadcast, "When Clemson players rub that Rock and run down the Hill, it's the most exciting 25 seconds in college football."

"Our entrance is different. That rock is something different than what most people have. To have something that is unique. To have something that is yours, it is a signature that no one else has. Everybody knows what team that is," former Clemson All-American Levon Kirkland said.

7

The Story of the Clemson Tiger Paw

I t does not take too long for a visiting team or its fans to know they are in Clemson, South Carolina.

Whether you're coming down Anderson Highway off Interstate 85 at exit 19B or coming from Greenville by way of Highway 123, the orange tiger paws on the road lead the way to Clemson.

Clemson's Tiger Paw is everywhere these days. And it's not just in Clemson. It is one of the more recognizable brands in college athletics, especially in college football. The tiger paw can be seen just about anywhere in the country and, in some occasions, overseas. Clemson alumni and Tiger fans love to wear their orange and love to show off the tiger paw.

Though the tiger paw is just as much a part of Clemson's rich traditions and history as anything else, it is still very young. The Clemson Tiger Paw turned fifty years old on July 21, 2020.

The idea of the Clemson Tiger Paw began with the retirement of legendary head coach Frank Howard following the 1969 football season. Clemson was trying to change its image. It was thinking forward, and since Clemson was welcoming in a new coach and a new era, the school thought it should change its image as well.

The late Dr. Robert C. Edwards, then president at Clemson, was the mastermind behind this upgrade. He hired an advertising firm—Henderson Advertising Co. out of Greenville—to come in and assist with helping the university find a new look. "We have asked these people to come in and help us examine and evaluate our program," Edwards said in the 1991 book

Death Valley Days. "In fact, they are helping us with a positive approach on all communication matters university-wide."

Clemson was changing its uniform and logo, and Edwards wanted something that would complement the school's nickname: the Tigers.

John Antonio, who worked for Henderson and passed away in 2013, wrote to every school in the country that used "Tiger" as its nickname and asked if they would send a picture of its logo. After most of them responded, Antonio discovered that a tiger is a tiger regardless if it was a Persian tiger, Bengal tiger or Sumatran tiger. "I found 32 schools with Tigers, and every one of them used the same picture," Antonio told the *Greenville News* in 1999. "One company made the decal and it went to everyone. There was no individuality. At the time colleges just put the school name or initials on their helmets."

Antonio came up with an idea of using a phantom tiger that left its paw prints wherever it went. After this discovery, Antonio came up with the idea of getting an impression of a real tiger's paw. But where were they going to find one?

The Henderson Agency wrote to the Field Museum in Chicago and asked for a plaster of Paris cast of the imprint of a tiger's paw. Before it was presented to the Clemson committee working with Henderson, Antonio's team made the imprinted paw print and tilted it about ten degrees to the right. The committee loved it.

On July 21, 1970, the Clemson Tiger Paw was born. The university not only put it on the football team's helmet and jersey, they also placed it on every athletic team's uniform, schedule cards, bumper stickers, pocket watches and the basketball court and the football field. And the letter *o* in Clemson was replaced with the paw.

New football coach Hootie Ingram, basketball coach Tates Locke, along with All-ACC running back Ray Yauger and Wright Bryan, Clemson's vice-president of development at the time, toured the state of South Carolina, introducing Clemson's new look to the media and Tiger fans. "Symbols like the tiger paw won't help us to win football games," Ingram was quoted as saying in *Death Valley Days*, "but we hope they will help retain the enthusiasm Clemson people are known for."

According to Ingram, Edwards, Locke and legendary baseball coach Bill Wilhelm did not like the tiger paw at first. But College Football Hall of Famer Frank Howard was a fan from the start, and that helped Ingram get everyone else on board.

Clemson fans took to the paw fast, as it was cast on every souvenir and clothing item one could find in Clemson.

By 1977, when Clemson started to make a splash on the national stage again, the paw was everywhere. Later that year, when Clemson fans headed to the Gator Bowl in Jacksonville, Florida, one student made a twenty-two-by-twenty-four-inch stencil of the paw. Every five miles or so, he painted a paw on the road for all Clemson fans to see as they were traveling to Jacksonville.

When Clemson played Nebraska for the national championship in the 1982 Orange Bowl, the tiger paws were extended all the way to Miami.

These days, the paw is everywhere, and every time someone sees the orange tiger paw, there is no doubt who it belongs to. "I didn't create the image of the of Bengal tiger, that came from the Smithsonian Institute. I created the use of it," Antonio said to the *Greenville News*. "I have always liked it because of its simplicity. Anyone can draw it. You can print it on the highway or your cheek. Regardless of size, it does not lose its identity. It evokes a positive emotional response. And it has passed the test of time."

And it symbolizes all that is Clemson University.

THE TRADITION OF CLEMSON'S TWO-DOLLAR BILL

Though Clemson fans will not give Georgia Tech the same credit as they give their foes to the south in Columbia, South Carolina, the Yellow Jackets are as true a rival of the Tigers as are the Gamecocks. The love-hate relationship and the back-and-forth between the two schools goes all the way back to the John Heisman days, when Georgia Tech stole the Hall of Fame coach from Clemson. Before Heisman went to Atlanta, the Tigers beat up on those "city boys" quite regularly. In fact, Clemson won six of the first eight meetings between the two schools, posting a 6-1-1 record. The two years that Heisman coached against Georgia Tech, Clemson won, 44–5, in 1902 and then 73–0 in 1903.

Tech was tired of losing, particularly of being embarrassed by "those country boys" from the Upstate of South Carolina. Georgia Tech was determined to draw Heisman away from Clemson. At the time, Heisman was making $1,800 a year at Clemson. Tech upped the ante and offered him $2,250 a year plus 30 percent of the gate receipts. It was an offer that was too good for Heisman to turn down.

In his first two years in Atlanta, Heisman's new team tied the Tigers in 1904 and then finally beat them the next year. But even without Heisman, the Clemson football program continued to soar, and in 1906, the Tigers beat their old head coach, 10–0. They then won again in 1907, this time, a 6–5 victory. In those days, touchdowns were worth five points.

However, Clemson's domination of the Yellow Jackets took an unfortunate turn in the spring of 1908, and it had nothing to do with football. Instead, it was an April Fools' joke that turned the Tigers' fortune around. April 1, 1908, is simply known in Clemson as the day of the "Pendleton Escapade."

In the 1991 book *Death Valley Days*, the story is told that, several years prior to 1908, many members of the student body cut class on April Fools' Day and went four miles down the road to the small town of Pendleton and killed the day playing jokes on each other. The day was all in fun. There was no destructive behavior by any of the cadets.

Then, in the summer of 1907, a new commandant of cadets came to Clemson and announced well in advance that there would be no toleration of anyone who cut classes on April 1, 1908. Like young people do, a good number of cadets defied the commandant's order. They cut school and went to Pendleton.

As Clemson was a military school, the commandant had the last say. The prank resulted in the expulsion of 306 cadets, including many of the football players. The football program did not recover from the blow for twenty years. At Clemson, it is simply known as the "Dark Ages" of Clemson football.

With Clemson falling, Heisman began to turn around the fortunes of Georgia Tech. The Yellow Jackets took advantage of the Tigers' bad luck and replaced them as a power in the South. In 1908, Heisman's Jackets beat Clemson, 30–6, and he never lost again to the Tigers. He won his last nine games against his old school before leaving Georgia Tech for Penn following the 1919 season.

From that point, Tech always felt like it was superior to Clemson, and the series record reflected it. From 1908 to 1969, Clemson won just three of the thirty-one meetings. During much of that time, Tech became a national power, winning six national championships.

Though for years the Tigers wanted the Yellow Jackets to play at Clemson, the Georgia Tech boosters and the school administrators felt they were too good to come to little ol' Clemson. Frank Howard was okay with it, though. He used it to his advantage and always got the football program a nice payday out of it.

Finally, in 1974, Howard and Georgia Tech athletic director Bobby Dodd agreed that the Yellow Jackets would play at Clemson that season. The Tigers, led by All-American tight end Bennie Cunningham, beat the Jackets, 21–17.

The two teams returned to playing in Atlanta from 1975 to 1977. The Tigers lost a close game to Tech in 1975 and tied them in 1976. They were expected to play again in Atlanta in 1978. However, Georgia Tech head coach Pepper Rodgers saw that Clemson's football program was turning the corner, and he did not want to play the Tigers anymore. When he learned that Howard and Dodd had a handshake agreement to play the proposed 1978 game and nothing had been signed, Rodgers got Tech to back out of the arrangement. So, the 1977 game was to be the last time the two programs played. Clemson athletic director Bill McLellan did all he could to reach an agreement between the two schools, but the series was broken off.

At the time, IPTAY's executive secretary, George Bennett, wanted to show businesses and the Atlanta Chamber of Commerce how much of an impact the Clemson fan base and alumni made on the local economy when they came to town. "We weren't going to any bowl games in that time, so this was our big game of the year," Bennett recalled. "We are going to Atlanta and we are going to have a good time.

"We were taking 15,000 to 17,000 people down there for that weekend and our people would go down there on Wednesday and the wives would shop and all this kind of stuff and stay at those fancy hotels and all of that. We really enjoyed going down there."

That's when Bennett came up with an idea that has turned into one of the more unique traditions in college football: Clemson's two-dollar bill. "I got the idea and went to Charlie Pell [Clemson's head coach] and said, 'Here is what we need to do if it is okay with you. We are going to take two-dollar bills down there and we are going to show the people in Atlanta how much money they are missing by doing this.' We publicized, wrote letters about it, put it in the IPTAY Report and told them to take two-dollar bills with them," Bennett said.

The Clemson fans did not let Bennett down. Tiger fans covered the city with two-dollar bills. They paid for their hotel rooms with two-dollar bills. They shopped using the bills, and they paid for all of their meals with two-dollar bills. It became such a story that the *Atlanta Journal-Constitution* wrote several articles about it, and local television stations reported on it as well.

The two-dollar bill was first commissioned in 1862 and has not been issued since 2003. When one makes its way into a business, the owner of the shop, restaurant or hotel is going to notice. It is going to leave an impression. "The waitresses in the hotels and restaurants were talking about it. Cab drivers, bellhops and all of that," Bennett said while laughing. "Pepper Rodgers told me in Memphis several years later that was the best promotion that he had ever heard. He said, 'You really got your point across to the people in Atlanta and to Georgia Tech and how much money they were going to be missing.'"

Georgia Tech joined the ACC in 1979, and the series with Clemson resumed in 1983 with Tech making a visit to Death Valley. The two teams are now cross-divisional rivals in the ACC and play home-and-home games every year.

As for the two-dollar bills, Clemson fans turned it up a notch. They used them later in 1977, when the Tigers went to the Gator Bowl in Jacksonville, Florida. It was Clemson's first bowl appearance in eighteen years. When the team went back to the Gator Bowl in 1978, Clemson fans started stamping the tiger paw on the bills so that local business new exactly where the bills came from. "We had so much fun with it," Bennett said.

Clemson fans buy Tiger Paw stamps at most shops in downtown Clemson or order them online. Bennett says he takes anywhere from $200 to $300 in $2 bills stamped with tiger paws when the Tigers play in a bowl game. Local banks in Clemson stock up in advance for the bill requests, especially when the Tigers are predicted to have a special season.

When Clemson played Notre Dame in the Cotton Bowl Classic in December 2018, Tiger fans flooded the Dallas–Fort Worth area with two-dollar bills. They did the same in San Francisco a few weeks later, when Clemson played Alabama in the national championship game.

Bennett enjoys the tradition as much as anyone and recalls a trip to Miami for the 2014 Orange Classic, when an Italian man gave him a 100-euro bill for a Clemson $2 bill. "We were checking into the Fontainebleau Hotel down there, and I am passing out two-dollar bills to everyone behind the counter that were checking us in, and all of sudden this little guy comes up and he starts jabbering," Bennett said. "I did not know what in the heck he was talking about. So, the girl behind the counter said, 'He wants one of your two-dollar bills.' So, I just whipped one out. I did not know who he was. It turns out he was Italian. So, I gave him a two-dollar bill. He gave me a one hundred-euro bill. My wife cashed that thing in the next day for a hundred and twenty-nine dollars.

"I started telling that story around the lobby and the hotel people were like, 'Where is that guy? Where is he? Where is he?'"

Clemson no longer has to use $2 bills to show what kind of impact it can make on a local economy, but the tradition carries on. Some Tiger fans take $2 bills with them on road trips during the regular season and, of course, to bowl games.

"We have had a lot of fun with it, and it has kind of identified Clemson with other people now, and they get excited about doing it," Bennett said.

9

THE CLEMSON-CAROLINA RIVALRY

IT'S JUST GOOD, OLD-FASHIONED HATE

The Clemson-Carolina rivalry—or Carolina-Clemson rivalry, depending on what side of the fence you are on—dates back long before anything happened on the gridiron. In fact, the bitterness between the two schools and their alumni goes back before Clemson even existed.

It all started when Benjamin Tillman, a farmer from Edgefield, South Carolina, was not pleased with the way the University of South Carolina was handling its agriculture department and demanded the university take agriculture more seriously.

Tillman, who became the governor of South Carolina in 1890, eventually, through the nastiness of politics, got his way. He was aided by Thomas Green Clemson, who had willed his Fort Hill estate to the state of South Carolina with the sole purpose of establishing a land-grant college, the Clemson Agricultural College of South Carolina.

When Clemson opened its doors in 1893, it nearly forced South Carolina to close its. South Carolina lost its university status and went back to being called South Carolina College. Tillman threatened to close the school, but he succeeded only in making it a liberal arts college while in office.

Though it had nothing to do with football, Tillman's feud with South Carolina planted the seed of hatred these two bitter rivals share today. The disdain between Clemson and South Carolina has lived out on the football field several times during their 117 years and has even gone into the streets.

Following the 1902 game, there was the near-shootout between the Clemson cadets and South Carolina students over a picture that showed a gamecock crowing over a sad tiger.

The cadets had warned the USC students, following the Gamecocks' 12–6 victory, not to bring the picture to the Elks' parade the following day. The USC students did not listen, so more than four hundred Clemson cadets marched on to the campus—with guns, keep in mind—demanding that the Carolina students hand over the picture.

Eventually, cooler heads prevailed after the police arrived. A joint committee of six students from both sides worked out a peaceful solution. The picture was burned between the two groups.

Due to the seriousness of what happened in 1902, the rivalry was suspended and not renewed until 1909. Since then, the Clemson-Carolina game has been played every year, with the 2019 contest being the 111th consecutive meeting. It is the second-longest uninterrupted series in college football.

The End of Big Thursday

The Clemson-Carolina game grew to be an important social and political event. From the first time the two met in 1896 until the 1959 meeting, they played in Columbia during the week of the South Carolina State Fair. The first fifty-seven meetings were played on the third Thursday of every October.

The game became so big, it was known as "Big Thursday" in the state of South Carolina. It was a holiday in the state. Students from both schools got out of class, and there was no business by the state government. All state offices were closed.

Clemson would hold its annual Gamecock burial the Tuesday night before the game, while South Carolina fans hosted their annual Tiger Burn at the steps of the statehouse. On game day, men and women dressed in their Sunday best, no matter the temperature. It became an attraction, a party if you will. Drinking and socializing became the norm on Big Thursday.

However, the novelty of the game started to wear off by the 1950s, and though the people of South Carolina loved Big Thursday, interest in college football was not quite the same after the rivalry game was over each year. "Big Thursday had been a tradition for 45 years before World War II and

Frank Howard blows a kiss goodbye to Big Thursday following Clemson's 27–0 victory over South Carolina in 1959. *Clemson Athletic Communications.*

16 years afterwards," longtime Clemson sports information director and Hall of Famer Bob Bradley said in the 1983 book *The Clemson Tigers: From 1896 to Glory.* "But that Thursday didn't work after a while because once the game was over, there was no football interest left in the state. There were still college and high school games to play, but the interest just wasn't the same."

The game was also wearing on the Tigers. Clemson head coach Frank Howard and college officials were not having as much fun as South Carolina was, though Clemson owned a 33-21-3 advantage in those first 57 meetings.

Clemson wanted the game to be moved to a home-and-home series. "We always had to sit in the sun, and we got tired of going down there every year," Howard said. "We weren't getting half of the tickets, half of the program and concession sales, and it knocked one game out of our schedule because we could not play the Saturday before or the Saturday after the Thursday game."

Clemson also made additions to Memorial Stadium in 1958 and 1960, so the seating capacity was comparable to Carolina Stadium in Columbia.

The last Big Thursday game was played on October 22, 1959. Clemson, on its way to another ACC Championship and a No. 12 ranking in the final AP Poll, beat the Gamecocks, 27–0. At the end of the game, *The State* newspaper photographer asked Howard if he would be willing to look out over Carolina Stadium and blow a kiss, symbolizing Clemson kissing Big Thursday goodbye. The picture is one of the more iconic images in the history of the rivalry.

VICTORY CIGARS AND "THE CATCH"

It all started following Clemson's 7–6 victory over Georgia in Athens. As the Tigers were making the seventy-mile hike back to Clemson, head coach Charlie Pell asked the bus driver to pull over. Pell wanted to savor the victory, considering it was Clemson's first win at Georgia since 1914.

So, as the legend goes, Pell went into a convenience store and bought every player on the team a cigar to commemorate the win. The cigar celebration became a big part of the 1977 season, and the Tigers used the Georgia win to jump-start a great run.

Pell and the Tigers went on to win seven straight games, and after each victory, they lit up a cigar. Well, sort of. Clemson wide receiver Jerry Butler chose not to smoke his cigars and instead he inscribed the score and the date on each of his. There was just one place left in his collection back at his dorm: the South Carolina game.

But South Carolina wanted no part of this so-called rite of passage. The Gamecocks were still smarting from the previous year's loss in Clemson, when the Tigers, despite winning just two games, pounded USC, 28–9, while knocking it out of contention for a possible Peach Bowl bid.

The roles were reversed this time around when they met in Columbia on November 19, 1977. The Gamecocks were sitting at 5-5 and knew their season was over regardless of the outcome, but Clemson, 7-2-1, was in the running for a Gator Bowl invitation and needed a victory over their archrival to secure the bid and go bowling for the first time since 1959.

During the first two and a half quarters, everything was pretty much going according to plan. The Tigers had a veteran team that was hungry and a head coach who had them believing in themselves. The Gamecocks were young and unsure of what they could accomplish.

The Tigers jumped out to a 17–0 lead by halftime, thanks to a Warren Ratchford touchdown, a 30-yard field goal by Obed Ariri and a Lester Brown

Chase Brice came off the bench for an injured Trevor Lawrence to lead Clemson to a come-from-behind win over Syracuse in 2018. The Clemson Insider.

Clemson players carry Danny Ford off the field after the Tigers beat Ohio State in the 1978 Gator Bowl. It was Ford's first game as a head coach. *Clemson Athletic Communications*.

Danny Ford speaks with his offensive line during the 1978 Gator Bowl. *Clemson Athletic Communications*.

Ken Hatfield (*center*) and Rodney Blunt (*33*) wait on the sideline as the final seconds run down in Clemson's win over South Carolina in 1990. Hatfield was 3-1 against the Gamecocks. *Clemson Athletic Communications*.

Dabo Swinney celebrates a big stop by his defense in the Tigers' win over Alabama in the 2019 CFP National Championship. The Clemson Insider.

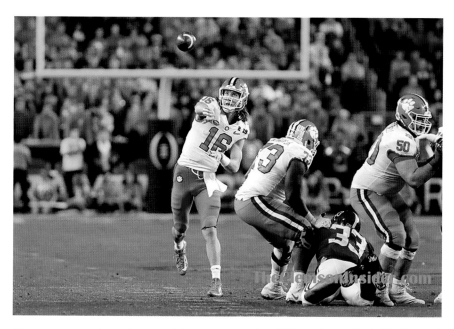

Trevor Lawrence threw three touchdown passes against Alabama in the 2019 CFP National Championship. The Clemson Insider.

All-American linebacker Isaiah Simmons following a tackle for a loss against South Carolina in the 2019 game in Columbia. The Clemson Insider.

Danny Ford was 96-29-4 in eleven full seasons at Clemson. *Clemson Athletic Communications*.

Danny Ford cheers on his team. *Clemson Athletic Communications.*

Deshaun Watson dives for the end zone during the Tigers' win over rival South Carolina in 2015. The Clemson Insider.

Deshaun Watson and Dabo Swinney embrace following the Tigers' win over Alabama in the 2017 CFP National Championship Game. The Clemson Insider.

Dabo Swinney and defensive coordinator Brent Venables look on during the Tigers' win over Ohio State in the Fiesta Bowl. The Clemson Insider.

Frank Howard visiting his rock after his retirement from Clemson in 1971. *Clemson Athletic Communications*.

Dabo Swinney talks to ESPN's Rece Davis following Clemson's 35–31 win over Alabama in the 2017 CFP National Championship. The Clemson Insider.

In 2018, Clemson quarterback Trevor Lawrence became the first freshman quarterback to lead his team to a national championship since 1985. The Clemson Insider.

touchdown from the 1-yard line. When fullback Ken Callicutt rumbled 52 yards midway through the third quarter, Clemson found itself up 24–0 and well on its way to victory. "I wouldn't say we thought we had it won, but it certainly felt like we did," quarterback Steve Fuller said. "It seemed like we were the far superior team for three and a half quarters."

It was about that time when South Carolina's Spencer Clark raced untouched for a 77-yard touchdown to cut the lead to 24–7. Over the next eight minutes, the Tigers could do nothing right and USC could do no wrong.

On Clemson's next three possessions, it fumbled the ball, went three-and-out and shanked a punt 10 yards. USC took advantage of each mistake to crawl back in the game with two Steve Dorsey touchdowns to make the score 24–20. South Carolina again gained possession of the football and had a chance to take the lead for the first time all night. "We called a pass route we had not run all day," South Carolina receiver Phil Logan said years later to *The State* newspaper in Columbia. "The defensive back backpedaled, and I curled."

When Logan curled, quarterback Ron Bass delivered a strike. It was fourth and 10 at the Clemson 40-yard line, and USC seemed desperate to make one last play to at least extend the drive. What Logan did not expect was to be so wide open. "I expected to be hit, but nobody was there," he said. "I cut across the field, got some blocks and I was never touched."

Logan's 40-yard touchdown gave the Gamecocks a 27–24 lead with 1:48 to play. Logan and his teammates were so confident the game was over that he was seen lifting his jersey to the crowd, revealing a garnet T-shirt with white letters: "No Cigar Today." "That kind of ticked this old boy off," Butler said.

It appeared to tick off the entire Clemson offense. Facing a third down and 7, Fuller hit Rick Weddington for 26 yards and a first down. After an incompletion, he found Dwight Clark across the middle for 18 yards, setting Clemson up at the USC 20.

"That was one of those games you can put on tape and watch, and it is still exciting," Fuller said. "You kind of feel like you don't know what the outcome is going to be even though it is obvious that you do. I remember watching it from an end zone camera and seeing how close fingers and hands were to tipping balls or somebody on their side making a good play. It makes you think 'Holy Mack! It is a miracle that it happened.'"

The Tigers quickly rushed to the line to run another play when Fuller noticed that South Carolina's defense was confused and having trouble getting players onto the field. The play called for Butler to cut to the corner,

Jerry Butler makes a twisting grab in the final minutes for the game-winning touchdown in Clemson's dramatic win over the Gamecocks in 1977. *Clemson Athletic Communications.*

but USC got pressure to Fuller and forced him to throw the ball earlier than he would have liked. "It was not a throwaway, but it was certainly a throw that was designed that nobody could have a chance to touch it but him," Fuller said.

Butler thought Fuller was throwing the ball away, but he was determined not to let that happen. "I saw the ball headed toward the middle of the field," he said. "He was dumping the ball out of the end zone, but I jumped and got my hands on the ball, and if I got my hands on the ball, I caught it."

Butler made a leaping, twisting catch that no one else could have made.

At Clemson, it is known simply as "The Catch."

"With all the great success lately, it is really nice for it to stand the test of time," Fuller said. "I think it was a moment in our history that probably is as big of a moment as any other. If we would have lost that game, it would have been like we made some progress, but really when it comes down to it, we really can't win the game we need to win. It would not have been starting over, but it certainly would have set us back. The fact that it was Carolina, that would have probably set us back for quite a while."

Instead, "The Catch" took the Tigers back to a bowl game for the first time in eighteen years and sent Clemson football into a new era, setting it up for its first run to a national championship four years later.

THE BIRTH OF THE ORANGE PANTS

One of the best-kept secrets in Clemson's storied history came in 1980. The funny thing is that the secret had nothing to do with a coaching change, an injury or anything of that nature. Instead, one of the best-orchestrated secrets to come out of the Clemson Athletic Department revolved around pants. That is right, pants. In particular, they were the orange pants.

It was in the summer of 1980 when the idea of the Clemson football team wearing orange pants presented itself to equipment manager Len Gough. That summer, he received several samples of orange plants from several distributers.

Gough, a 1975 graduate of Clemson, was fascinated by the orange pants, and he thought they could be used in some way, but he wasn't exactly sure how the team would use them. He brought the idea up to head coach Danny Ford, who liked the idea, but maybe not for the 1980 season.

After his meeting, Gough did not hear from Ford about the pants for a couple of months. Then one day, Ford made his way down to the equipment room prior to the Tigers' game against Virginia Tech and asked if it was possible to have them available for the South Carolina game, which was seven weeks away. "I could not give him an answer right away, but we thought we should ask a couple of the players, some we could trust with a secret," Gough explained in the 2016 book *If These Walls Could Talk: Stories of the Clemson Tigers*.

Ford chose two of Clemson's most respected players and team leaders, safety Willie Underwood and linebacker Jeff Davis. "We were totally caught off guard," Davis said. "We had no idea, but we liked them."

Ford told Davis and Underwood they might wear the orange pants against South Carolina in the regular-season finale, but the pants were to be a surprise. The players were not to tell anyone about them. The two did not tell anyone, sort of. Davis let the cat out of the bag to his longtime roommate, wide receiver Perry Tuttle. But he made Tuttle swear to secrecy. Tuttle did not say a word. The secret was safe.

Ford finally gave Gough the go-ahead to order the pants the Monday after a 35–33 win at Wake Forest. That was on November 3, 1980, nineteen days before the Tigers were to host South Carolina at Death Valley. At the time, Ford knew his team was going to need a boost to beat the Gamecocks. They were having a great season in Columbia and were likely headed to the Gator Bowl, while running back George Rogers was on his way to winning the Heisman Trophy.

At the time that Ford finally made the decision to order the orange pants, Clemson was 5-3 with a home game against No. 14 North Carolina that

Danny Ford and Perry Tuttle (*far right*) were joined by former Nebraska head coach Tom Osborne and running back Mike Rozier (*far left*) on the *Today Show* on NBC in December 1981. *Clemson Athletic Communications.*

same week and then a date at Maryland before the annual grudge match against a ranked South Carolina squad. "We were needing something," Ford said. "We were stuck in a .500 year with an important game. Momentum was probably not on our side. It was not a good week going into that game and probably needed all the help we could get."

Gough knew they were going to be cutting it close, so he got the assistance of head trainer Fred "Doc" Hoover. Hoover was friends with Hank Spiers, the vice-president of Russell Mills in Alexander, Alabama. They had nineteen days to make 120 pants. But the cloth to make the pants did not end up at the plant until November 19, three days before the South Carolina game. Russell Mills told Gough the pants would be ready on Friday, the day before the game, so he and pilot Eddie Ambrose flew to Alexander to pick up the pants.

The orange pants were still a secret to the majority of the team and those in the Clemson athletic office, as just ten people knew what Gough and Ford were trying to pull off. When Gough and the pilot reached Alexander, the pants were still not ready. In fact, they were not ready until 3:00 p.m., twenty-two hours before kickoff.

After finally getting the pants back to Clemson, Gough and assistant equipment manager Bobby Douglas washed the pants. At seven o'clock the next morning, they came in and put identifications on each pair. Though they had just six hours before kickoff, they did it by themselves—the secret had gone on for so long, they did not want a student manager to ruin the surprise.

Meanwhile, back at the team hotel in Anderson, the team was finishing its pregame breakfast when Ford got up and spoke to the players. "We knew something was up, but we didn't really know what," said running back Cliff Austin.

A lot of the guys on the team thought Ford was going to tell them he was stepping down as head coach, because following the Tigers' 34–7 loss at Maryland, rumors had circulated that Ford was out as head coach. Instead, Ford pulled out a pair of the orange pants. "When he did that, the room went crazy," Davis said. "That's all the guys could talk about was wearing those orange pants with the orange jersey and the orange helmet and how the fans were going to love it. Coach Ford was a master motivator. He knew how to push the right buttons.

"That moment relaxed us. All of sudden, we weren't thinking about having to win this game to save his job or about how we were going to stop George Rogers or any of that. We were just looking forward to playing the game."

Back in Clemson, there was still a few hours before kickoff, and Gough and Douglas had already snuck the pants into the locker room, where the managers hung them up in the lockers beside the white pairs of pants. The players were to warm up in the white pants to make sure the sixty-four thousand fans, as well as the Gamecocks, did not suspect a thing.

Everything was going to plan until one of the managers brought a man by the name of Paul Coakley into the locker room. Coakley worked for Clemson and was there to pick something up. "I felt bad for him, but we had to keep him in the locker room until we left the last time," Gough said. Gough said Coakley's eyes grew twice their size when he saw the orange pants. They could not risk him telling someone what was going on, because it could get back to the Gamecocks. So, Gough put him in Ford's interview room for the next hour.

With Coakley secured, the rest of pregame went off without a hitch. The team left the field from warmups five minutes earlier than normal so that they had enough time to change into the orange pants. None of the sixty-four thousand fans at Memorial Stadium or the South Carolina squad had a clue about what was going to happen. "I never quite thought it would have the reaction that it had on the players that it had," Ford said.

To keep as many fans as possible from seeing the Tigers load the buses in the orange pants to be transported to the top of the hill, Ford had the bus pull up next to the door where recruits hung out. So, the players went through the recruits' room to get on the buses.

When Clemson got to the top of the hill, the players stayed on the buses until the Gamecocks came out onto the field. They wanted them to see what was about to happen. They wanted them to feel the fans' enthusiasm.

When the Tigers finally made it to the top of the hill, dressed in all-orange for the first time, Death Valley became deafening. "When the fans saw us, they absolutely went crazy," Davis said. "We knew we were going to win."

It did not appear as if Clemson was going to win late in the third quarter, when the Gamecocks drove the football to the Clemson 16 and was in position to take their first lead of the day. But with thirty-two seconds remaining in the quarter, Underwood stepped in front of a Garry Harper pass and raced 64 yards down the sideline before stepping out of bounds at the USC 24. Six plays later, quarterback Homer Jordan called his own number from the 1-yard line as the Tigers took a 13–6 lead.

Though Rogers carried the ball 28 times for 168 yards, Clemson kept him out of the end zone. "I told Jim Carlen, who became a good friend of mine after we both got out of coaching…I told him, and I told George Rogers this

Willie Underwood (20) celebrates with his teammates after an interception in the 1980 Clemson-Carolina game. The Tigers broke out the orange pants for the first time in the 1980 game. *Clemson Athletic Communications.*

many times, but there is no telling how bad they would have beat us, orange pants or no orange pants, if they gave the ball to George Rogers on every play." But they didn't.

On South Carolina's next possession, Harper again tried to go outside with a pass, but the pass was again cut off by Underwood, who this time made sure he did not step out of bounds as he raced 37 yards down the sideline for a touchdown, giving Clemson a 20–6 lead.

"For some reason they wanted to throw two out cuts and Willie Underwood picked them off," Ford said. "Mickey Andrews [Clemson's defensive coordinator] was still here then and he just completely believed that a strong safety could get underneath an out cut. That is a long way to travel. I never did believe he could get there if he threw the ball perfectly on the outside shoulder.

"He broke on the ball once and it looked like a replay the second time because it looked like the same play. He proved Mickey right. He could get underneath the out cut and he just turned the whole football game around. Still today, I don't think we beat them if they don't throw those two passes."

It was meant to be. Prior to the 1980 South Carolina game, Underwood did not have an interception in his first forty-six games at Clemson. In his last game in a Clemson uniform, he had two. Was it the orange pants?

Underwood finished the game with seventeen tackles and was named the National Player of the Week by *Sports Illustrated*. Clemson clinched its 27–6 victory over the Gamecocks when Jeff McCall went 15 yards for a touchdown late in the fourth quarter.

The win over the Gamecocks lifted Clemson to its perfect run in 1981, which ended with a 22–15 victory over Nebraska in the 1982 Orange Bowl, sealing the Tigers' first national championship in football.

Clemson went on to post a 16-2 record under Danny Ford when it wore orange pants.

The Ugliest Moment in the History of the Rivalry

There have been plenty of good things for Dabo Swinney to remember in his time at Clemson. He has won multiple national and ACC championships and has beat a few Hall of Fame head coaches along the way.

However, one of the images that haunt him to this day was seeing Lou Holtz, then the head coach at the University of South Carolina, holding on to the leg of one of his players as he did everything he could to break up a brawl that forever scarred the rivalry between Clemson and South Carolina. "Oh my," Swinney recalled. "This guy is fixing to get killed. It was total chaos,"

At the time, Swinney was Tommy Bowden's wide receiver coach and was finishing up his second season at Clemson. Swinney, who played at Alabama, knew all about hate in a rivalry game. He grew up in Alabama and played and coached in the Iron Bowl between Alabama and Auburn.

However, what happened on November 20, 2004, was something totally different and something he does not ever want to experience again.

The brawl broke out near the end of the Tigers' 29–7 victory at Memorial Stadium. The fight started when Clemson defensive end Bobby Williamson threw down South Carolina quarterback Syvelle Newton with 5:48 to play. Offensive lineman Chris White then pushed Williamson, and players rushed in from both sidelines. The fight stretched nearly 60 yards along the center of Frank Howard Field. Local and state authorities came on the field to separate players, and the game was delayed for nearly twenty minutes. "It was an embarrassing chapter for both schools," Bowden said.

The tension started in the stadium long before Williamson threw down Newton. As the Tigers were running down the hill prior to kickoff, Newton

Lou Holtz (*left*), who coached South Carolina from 1999 to 2004, and Tommy Bowden, who coached Clemson from 1999 to 2008, speak prior to the Tigers' 63–17 victory in 2003. *Clemson Athletic Communications.*

and several other USC players were taunting the Clemson players. A few guys, including tight end Ben Hall, did not like the gesture and confronted the Gamecocks. That led to some pushing and shoving. The SEC officiating crew did not help by allowing it all to happen without penalizing either team.

The bad blood carried over into the game, as both teams took cheap shots at one another without a personal-foul penalty called. As Clemson pulled away and took control of the game in the second half, the pushing and shoving got worse.

There was a lot of emotion in the stadium. Everyone knew Holtz planned to retire at the end of the season. The Gamecock players desperately wanted a bowl game to be the last game he coached in. They were already bowl eligible, but they were hoping that, with a win over Clemson, they could position themselves for a more prestigious bowl.

As for the Tigers, they were 5-5 and needed a win to become bowl eligible. The night before, the NBA's Detroit Pistons and Indiana Pacers had been in a fight when a fan threw beer on an Indiana player. The footage aired all night and all morning on ESPN's *SportsCenter*. It set the table for what Bowden called "the perfect storm."

Clemson running back Yusef Kelly, who was jumped from behind by a USC player while trying to break things up, was photographed kicking a South Carolina player on the ground and later throwing a Gamecock helmet into the stands. South Carolina players were punching Clemson players in the end zone while Clemson students leaned over the fence and encouraged the fight.

It was a moment that stained the rivalry. "This is the first time that this has ever happened to me in a football game," Holtz said. "There is no excuse, I take responsibility."

The following week, both Clemson and South Carolina officials agreed to turn down bowl invitations, while the ACC suspended six Clemson players for one game the following season. The SEC did the same to six Gamecocks.

Bowden calculated that the players lost about $2,000 in bowl stipends and gifts. Plus, it was the last college football game for the seniors on both sides. "It was a pretty strict punishment, but it helped us educate our players," he said.

WATSON BROUGHT THE RIVALRY BACK TO CLEMSON

Deshaun Watson limped onto the field at Memorial Stadium with an injured left knee and helped Clemson do something it had not achieved in the five previous years: earn a win over South Carolina.

Head coach Dabo Swinney announced in the moments after the game that Watson's feat was more courageous than everyone had thought. He took down the Gamecocks, not just on a bad knee, but on one that had a torn ACL.

Even with a torn left knee, the freshman quarterback threw for 269 yards and two touchdowns while running for two more in Clemson's 35–17 victory over South Carolina on November 29, 2014. "I wasn't really in a lot of pain. I just could not move it that much," Watson said afterward.

Watson went out of the game two times. On the Tigers' opening drive, after Clemson moved the football from its own 3 to the South Carolina 26, but following an incomplete pass to Germone Hopper, he took himself out of the game.

That drive ended with a missed field goal.

Leading 21–7 with just under three minutes to play in the first half, the Gainesville, Georgia native left the game again when the Tigers moved the

Deshaun Watson was 3-0 all-time against South Carolina, including a 35–17 win at Death Valley in 2014. He totaled four touchdowns and threw for 269 yards despite playing with a torn ACL. The Clemson Insider.

football to the USC 49. He took himself out of the game after running back Wayne Gallman ran off left guard for three yards.

Swinney said the brace was cutting off the circulation in Watson's calf, so they took him into the locker room just before the end of the first half, took the brace off and readjusted everything.

Watson returned in the third quarter and did not leave the game again. He led the Tigers to two more touchdowns after that, including running for a 1-yard score in the fourth quarter that sealed the victory. "Deshaun Watson, he is a mental and genetic freak. That's all I can say," Swinney said. "There is no other way I can say it to be honest with you. This kid just played this whole game with a torn ACL. And when he shot off and ran for that touchdown that was just unbelievable."

Watson did not actually score a touchdown on the play Swinney described, but it was a gutsy effort nonetheless. From the South Carolina 10, he ran 9 yards on a scramble that put the ball at the 1. He scored on the next play, his first of two rushing touchdowns. That gave the Tigers a 21–7 lead with 4:55 to play in the second quarter.

On that Saturday, Watson was about beating the Gamecocks and ending the five-game losing streak to Clemson's rivals. And with his 14-of-19 passing, he was one of the main reasons why. "He was great. I will tell you, I was amazed," Swinney said.

The win over the Gamecocks in 2014 was the first of six straight in the series by the Tigers heading into the 2020 season. It was a performance that not only snapped a five-game losing streak to South Carolina but also provided the first sign of the Tigers regaining control of the rivalry.

Starting with Watson's heroic afternoon, Clemson has outscored the Gamecocks 256–104. The six-game win streak is the second longest by either team in the series, bested only by the Tigers' seven-game win streak from 1934 to 1940. Heading into the 2020 game, Clemson has a commanding 71-42-4 record against the Gamecocks.

10

It All Started with Fuller

For nearly two months, assistant coach Harold Steelman drove to Spartanburg and back to Clemson four days a week to see Steve Fuller play baseball for his American Legion Post. Georgia assistant coach Frank Inman did the same from Athens, Georgia.

"Those two guys saw more bad American Legion Baseball games than they ever wanted to see," Fuller laughed.

It was mid-July, and fall camp was expected to begin in two weeks for colleges all across the country. However, Fuller, one of the nation's top recruits in 1975, had not decided on where he was going to play college football.

When the summer started, Georgia was the leader for Fuller's services. Fuller's brother was playing baseball for the Bulldogs, plus he knew a lot about the program. Vince Dooley was entering his twelfth season at Georgia and had already led the Bulldogs to two Southeastern Conference Championships. "They had what can be argued as a fairly significant national reputation. They were probably first on my list for quite a while," Fuller recalled.

Tennessee was a close second on the list. The Volunteers were led by Bill Battle, a young and energetic head coach who had won 72 percent of his games and was someone Fuller really liked. It also helped that they had Stanley Morgan on the team, who was from Easley, South Carolina, and was someone Fuller liked to watch.

Then there was Clemson.

The Tigers were led by Red Parker, who was entering his third season. They had All-American tight end Bennie Cunningham, who was from nearby Seneca, South Carolina, and were coming off a 7-4 season, the program's best since Frank Howard led them to the 1959 Bluebonnet Bowl.

"Clemson at that time was probably a distant third. I had them on my list because I had quite a few friends who were either going there or had been there and a lot of families in Spartanburg and Greenville areas were Clemson people," Fuller remembers. "I really didn't know that much about the program. Certainly, I knew who the coach was and who the good players were and all of that, but I really did not follow Clemson football."

However, during his senior year at Spartanburg High School, Fuller saw Steelman almost every day. When he came home from one of his many practices as a multisport athlete, Fuller was greeted by Steelman, who was waiting for him in the living room. "He was a little bit older fella. Most other programs were sending out their young go-getters as their recruiting guys, but they put Harold on me," Fuller said. "Coach Steelman spent a lot of time at my house in Spartanburg and with my parents and he became to me, really, I would not say a father figure, but he was an older guy that I really respected. He said and did everything in a really classy way. He was probably the one that started stirring me towards Clemson of anybody else."

Steelman's persistence paid off. Though he liked Battle, Tennessee just did not feel right, so Fuller eliminated the idea of signing with the Volunteers. Now it came down to Georgia and Clemson.

Georgia would be nice, Fuller thought, because his brother was a student-athlete there and he was familiar with everything. However, there was just something different about Clemson. There was something about it that made it feel right. "I just felt comfortable about staying in-state and at a school close to where I grew up. There was a lot of local support. I would not call it local pressure because it was just good solid support. I did not have a key moment or factor, it just felt right in my gut that it would be nice to stay in-state."

It did not hurt that Parker had a good second season in Tigertown, and with the list of recruits he was bringing in, Fuller could sense they were on to something special at Clemson. "The program was not thriving, but it was certainly on the way up," the quarterback recalled. "The '74 season they had a was fairly good year and I just felt like I would try to make it happen here in South Carolina."

When he finally settled with the Tigers, Fuller did not leave himself much wiggle room to work out. "They sent me the off-season workout program and it was a fairly significant notebook full of stuff, but I laugh about it because when I finally signed, 95 percent of that, all the dates and stuff, had already passed," Fuller chuckled as he told the story. "So, I really missed out on what they would expect out of a new recruit, to come in there already done and ready to go."

At the time, Fuller had no idea what coming to the Tigers meant to the Clemson program. There were no recruiting services back then. There were no star rankings, combines and national signing day shows where guys put on a hat for the camera on ESPN. "It was nothing like that. There weren't any fan sites where fans follow recruiting so closely and they know when a good recruit goes and visits somebody and deciding what it meant. Is it good for Clemson or bad for Clemson? It did not exist back then," Fuller said. "I did not think about it. I was obviously concerned with how it meant to me and my future. Obviously, I wanted to take Clemson to a higher level, but I did not think it was really an important thing."

But Fuller's decision to come to Clemson played a big role in who else came over the next decade, as Clemson became one of the premier programs in the country. Clemson legends like Bubba Brown, Randy Scott, Joe and Jeff Bostic, Dwight Clark, Jerry Butler, Jeff Davis and Perry Tuttle all wanted to play with Steve Fuller. His decision to come to Clemson in

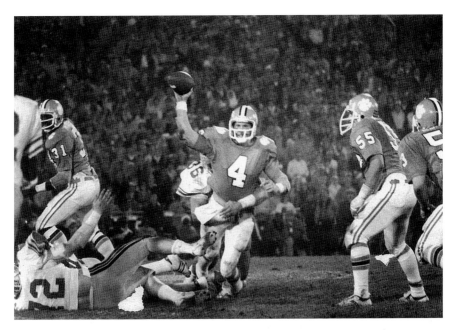

Steve Fuller gets off a pass during the Tigers' win over Ohio State in the 1978 Gator Bowl. *Clemson Athletic Communications.*

the summer of 1975 played a big role in the program's run to a national championship six years later.

"Red Parker does not get the credit he deserves for building this program," former Clemson head coach Danny Ford said. "He recruited all of those guys. He got them to come to Clemson. It's a shame he never got a chance to reap the benefits of it. He and his staff set us up for the run we went on in the late 1970s. It laid the foundation for what we were able to build on during our time there."

Despite the fact that Fuller had little opportunity to get ready for the 1975 season, he was such a rare talent that Parker wanted to get him on the field. He played in the Tigers' season opener against Tulane. Though the Tigers lost the game, 17–13, Fuller played well enough that Parker felt he should start when Clemson visited Alabama in Week 2.

"We ended up losing 56–0," Fuller laughed, "but it gets worse. We kicked off to them and we stopped them on the first series. But the punter kicks the ball about 70 yards, and it goes out of bounds on the half-yard line. So, my first snap as a Clemson starter, my feet were in the end zone in Tuscaloosa.

"They were really, really good that year. The good news, and bad news, is I broke my ankle on the second series, so I was done. Seventy-five to 80 percent of my freshman year was now done. In this day and age, I would have certainly redshirted because I played half of one game and one series of another game."

Fuller spent much of the rest of the year sitting on the sideline with a cast on his leg and watching the Tigers lose to almost everybody. "It was a struggle," he said.

Clemson finished the 1975 season 2-9, the worst for the program since it went 2-6-1 in 1952. It's also the last time any Clemson team won less than three games in a season. "We did have some injuries and we had a lot of freshman and sophomores playing. You could start to see some glimpses of some good things, but it still was not anything close to where we needed to be to beat good football teams," Fuller recalled.

Things began to change in the spring of 1976. For Fuller, he had to go out and try to win the job back. He got to a starter's level early in his freshman year, but after the injury, he sat out most of the rest of the year, with the exception of a few brief appearances at the end of the season.

"I had to go back out and win a job," he said. "I was really paying attention to what I was doing and working really hard. I think a lot of other guys were in that same boat. They got a little taste of what it was like and they knew what they had to do to get better. They knew what it took. They were playing against quality Division I guys, and they realized they were not quite to that level, not talent wise, but strength wise, experience wise and all of those things that you need.

"Our spring practice that year was a war. Coach Parker he was not pleased with 2-9 either, so he let it go. It was not one of these shoulder pads and shorts and seven-on-sevens. It was all out, 11-on-11, knocking the crap out of each other for 30 days. It was good."

However, the results did not show on the field. The Tigers had a difficult schedule once again. They were hammered by No. 9 Georgia, 41–0, in Week 2 of the season and then slid to 1-3-2 to open the year.

But following the loss to the Bulldogs, Clemson slowly started to show improvement. They tied Georgia Tech in Atlanta in Week 3, lost a nail-biter at Tennessee the following week and had Wake Forest on the ropes before suffering another difficult defeat on the road. They then came back home to tie Duke.

"It was very obvious that we had gotten better from our freshman year and things were looking up, maybe our time was coming. Then they fired our coaching staff," Fuller said.

In its final five games that year, Clemson went on to win two of them, as it beat Florida State on the road and later took down rival South Carolina, 28–9, in the season finale, knocking the Gamecocks out of a possible Peach Bowl bid.

The players had hoped beating the Gamecocks the way that they did was enough to save Parker's job. But it wasn't. Parker was fired the next week, and Charlie Pell, who was Parker's assistant coach head coach and defensive coordinator in 1976, was elevated to head coach.

"We felt bad because the guys that we worked with, that coached us, that recruited us, we knew their families, we knew where they lived, we had been in their homes…it is a difficult thing anytime a coaching staff is fired," Fuller explained. "Coach Pell had come into coach defense the previous year and we did not feel like that was fair, either. Coach Parker had taken all the lumps, and right when things looked like they were going to get a little better, he was going to miss out on all the good stuff.

"We could feel it, we could see it, there was too many good players that were running around. You knew it was going to happen, it was just a matter of when. We felt terrible that Coach Parker was not going to be a part of it. My coach, Don Murray, and Coach Steelman, who recruited me, all of these guys are gone."

But there was some good, too. Under Parker, Clemson was running the split-back veer, which was not really innovative and was not conducive to Fuller's skill level.

"The good news, as it turned out, was when Coach [Jimmye] Laycock came in with Coach Pell's group we changed the offense and I think that did make a difference for a lot of us. We were able to do more things on offense, which made us better players," Fuller remembered.

Laycock brought in the Power-I formation, which became Clemson's standard offense for many years under Pell and Ford. They ran the trap option out of the I-formation, but they also threw the ball a little more and ran a few more screens than they had under Parker.

"We were still running the option, but most of the stuff was not at the line of scrimmage. When you do split-back veer, everything is right at the line of scrimmage really quick. When it happens, it happens. Whereas with the I-formation there is a lot more reading going on," Fuller said. "For me personally, it gave me a chance to start reading coverages and reading defenses a little differently, which in the previous offense, you really did not do much of. I think it suited our personnel better. We had a really good offensive line and a couple of really good running backs and our receivers were excellent, so opening up the offense a little more was beneficial, and it proved out that way."

"Steve was really good in the I-formation because he could sprint out and throw on the run," Ford said. "He could roll, bootleg and run play action. He could also run the option. He was very versatile. In the split-veer, defenses could force you to do certain things and he was not the type that needed to be running the ball all the time. He did not need to be hit on because he was too valuable as a thrower. He also made good decisions and was a very smart kid and could really break down a defense."

Fuller does not remember much about how things went down in the off-season in 1977, but he does remember how players like left guard Steve Kenney, right guard Joe Bostic, tight end Dwight Clark, wide receiver Jerry Butler, linebacker Randy Scott, linebacker Bubba Brown and defensive back Rex Varn were starting to blossom and come into their own. "We had some really, really good players that Coach Parker had left here," said Ford, who was Pell's offensive line coach at Clemson in 1977 and '78. "We had a lot of good players. We had really, really good players when you compared them to Virginia Tech. We were not too far off from what we had at Alabama. We were blessed to come into a situation like we had here."

The Clemson players knew they could compete with teams like North Carolina, NC State and Maryland, who in those years owned the ACC.

Charlie Pell (*left*), Steve Fuller (*center*) and Danny Ford converse during Clemson's win at Georgia in 1977. *Clemson Athletic Communications.*

"They knew what it took, and they knew how to get there," Fuller said. "Everybody was working really hard. There was optimism that may not have been there when we first showed up. When there is a light at the end of the tunnel, guys work a little harder and they see a little bit of reward that is waiting on them."

The Tigers really proved to themselves that they could play with the big boys of the ACC in the season opener. Though they ultimately lost to No. 10 Maryland, 21–14, at Death Valley, they gained confidence in the game and felt like they were close to knocking down the door and beating a ranked team.

That happened in Week 2, when they went to Georgia and knocked off the 17th-ranked Bulldogs in Athens for the first time since 1914. Following the win over Georgia, the Tigers went on to win their next six games. The seven-game winning streak was the longest for the program since Frank Howard's 1950 and 1951 teams won nine straight games over the last six weeks of the 1950 season and the first three games of 1951.

It was the program's longest in-season win streak since the 1948 team went 11-0.

Then came the Notre Dame game at Death Valley. It was the first meeting between the two schools. The Irish, who went on to win the national championship that season, were ranked No. 5 in the country and were led by a young quarterback named Joe Montana. Clemson was ranked No. 15 in the polls, its highest ranking since it peaked at No. 8 in 1960.

"We completely dominated them and ran up and down the field for three and a half quarters," Fuller said. "But we figured out a way to lose that game. I go back and have nightmares. I fumbled one and Lester Brown fumbled one and they had Montana and he converted three or four third-down conversions on the last drive.

"We are up 17–7 late in the third and we are going in for another touchdown and we fumbled. All of that stuff at the time, it felt terrible, and then they turn out to win a share of the national championship that year. They become a national champion after we should have beat them by four touchdowns. But at that point and time, we knew at least talent wise, we could just about play with anybody."

Clemson went on to beat South Carolina in the season finale, thanks to Jerry Butler's miraculous catch, and accepted a bid to play Pittsburgh in the Gator Bowl. It marked the program's first bowl appearance in eighteen years. The Tigers finished the season 8-3-1, ranked 19th in the final Associated Press Poll and 2nd in the ACC with a 4-1-1 mark.

Charlie Pell is carried off the field following Clemson's 7–6 win at Georgia in 1977. It marked the Tigers' first win in Athens, Georgia, since 1914. *Clemson Athletic Communications.*

By the time 1978 rolled around, Fuller, along with fellow seniors like Bostic, Kenney, Butler, Clark, Steve Gibbs, Scott, Willie Jordan and Steve Ryan, felt it was a "last-stand kind of mentality."

After winning just two games in 1975, they finished only one game back of North Carolina from winning an ACC Championship in 1977. In the 1950s and '60s, Clemson owned the ACC, winning six league titles under legendary head coach Frank Howard from 1956 to 1967. Now they had their chance to grab the bull by the horns and take what many Clemson people feel is their birthright in college football.

"It was our last chance. It was our last opportunity," Fuller said. "We had a senior group that had really gone through the worst of times, had gotten better, had a couple of setbacks in the middle of it. This was really our time. We were either going to do it or don't do it."

Six players off the 1978 team—Butler, Fuller, Jim Stuckey, Jeff Bryant, Perry Tuttle and Terry Kinard—were first-round NFL draft choices.

Seventeen players were drafted and eighteen played in the NFL. Eleven of those 18 played at least five years in the NFL. "It was a last chance opportunity for our group," Fuller said. "We had been together and really suffered through a lot of this together, along with the fans and the support groups at Clemson. It was just time to step up and do it."

The expectations for Clemson to do it were extremely high heading into the 1978 season. For the first time since 1960, the Tigers opened the season in the preseason poll, ranked No. 18 by the Associated Press.

After rolling over the Citadel by a score of 58–3 in the season opener, they journeyed down the road to Athens in Week 2, when they faced an unranked Bulldogs team that was cranky from the year before. "We got knocked back. It was just a disappointing game," Fuller said. "They were awfully good, but they were not as good as we were. We knew that and it was a really big setback early on."

Georgia forced six turnovers that afternoon and kept the Tigers off the scoreboard while limiting the running game to 156 yards. In the end, despite a gritty effort by the defense, Clemson fell, 12–0.

Clemson did not take another opponent for granted the rest of the year. The Tigers steamrolled through their next six opponents, beating Villanova, Virginia Tech, Virginia, Duke, NC State and Wake Forest by an average margin of 27.7 points per game.

They then beat defending ACC champion North Carolina by four points, setting up a winner-take-all matchup with No. 11 Maryland in College Park, Maryland, on November 18, 1978. "After the Georgia game, it would have been easy to say, 'here we go again,' just waiting for bad things to happen, but we were a group that was not going to let it happen," Fuller said.

Winners of seven straight, the Tigers moved back into the top 20 after their win at NC State. By the time the Maryland game rolled around, they had moved up to No. 12. With the Terrapins at No. 11 in the AP Poll, it was the highest-ranked matchup between two ACC teams in the league's twenty-six-year history.

The game lived up to its championship billing.

"First of all, we were southern kids, and it was cold as hell," Fuller recalls about that championship game at Maryland. "Not that we were beach guys and could not handle it, but it was a cold day. Also, we were two really, really good football teams and they were excellent. If you looked at their schedule, they had beaten some really good teams, as we had.

"We knew going in that it was going to be difficult, but we felt like we were ready to make that step."

It was a game of big play after big play. At one point, there were three consecutive scores that covered at least 60 yards. Maryland scored on a blocked punt that was recovered in the end zone by Mike Carney. On the next possession, Jerry Butler got loose in the secondary and went 87 yards for a score.

The Terrapins countered with a 98-yard touchdown run by Steve Atkins, still the longest run in ACC history. But Clemson came right back as Fuller hit Clark over the middle and he raced 67 yards for a touchdown.

With the game tied at 21, the Tigers ended a 70-yard drive in the fourth quarter with a 5-yard Lester Brown touchdown for a 28–21 lead. But like it did the whole game, Maryland responded and drove to the Clemson 7-yard line.

However, on third down, Clemson's Bubba Brown stopped Maryland's Dean Richards for a loss, and the Terps settled for a field goal with 1:56 left. Chuck Rose recovered the ensuing onside kick, and Fuller guided the Tigers to a pair of first downs to run out the clock as the Tigers clinched the ACC Championship with a 28–24 victory.

It was Clemson's first league title since 1967.

"We just needed to make a first down. If we make a first down, we win the conference and we put a lot of the ghosts to bed," Fuller said. "They have literally…and if you remember anything about Coach Pell and Coach Ford and any of those guys. We were not going to throw the ball. It was not going to happen.

"So, we literally lined everybody up eleven-on-eleven. They had everybody up and we had everybody tight in there. We are going to run the ball three times and make a first down, or you are going to stop us. That's kind of how it was. I remember Marvin Sims, I think we ran option, and I gave it to him on the inside and he busted a tackle and got the first down. That was probably the most important three-yard run in a long, long time at Clemson."

After the game, Clemson accepted a bid to play Ohio State in the Gator Bowl.

"It was a little bit of a disappointment because we went into the locker room after the game, we felt like we were headed to the Orange Bowl, which at that point and time was the big bowl," Fuller said. "It turns out we already made some kind of commitment to the Gator Bowl, again. We were not disappointed, but it was kind of a little bit of a letdown.

"As it worked out, the Maryland game was an early afternoon game and by the end of the day on that Saturday, we would have gotten to the Orange Bowl, and it may have given us a chance to play for a national championship, but it did not turn out that way."

The Tigers' disappointment did not last long, because when their plane landed in Greenville several hours later, there were thousands and thousands of people greeting them at the airport. "We had never seen anything like that," Fuller said. "We always had great fan support, but the Clemson people basically shut down the airport. It was a great, great moment."

More than eight thousand fans greeted the Tigers, as cars parked up and down both sides of the road, as Clemson fans made their way for more than a mile from the airport to Interstate 85. "We saw a lot of people, but we really did not understand what was happening until we got out. The Greenville Airport was not that big at the time, but it was jammed full of Clemson folks," Fuller recalled. "It was a homecoming you can't ever imagine. For us it was something we never experienced before. It was fabulous."

The Tigers carried the momentum and their renewed sense of enthusiasm from the Greenville Airport to the next week, when they closed the regular season against rival South Carolina. When he was a freshman, Fuller remembered the looks on the seniors' faces in Columbia that year when the Gamecocks beat them as bad as they did.

After winning the previous two meetings against USC, Fuller and the rest of the seniors were ready to hand the Gamecocks some payback, which they did in an easy 41–23 victory at Death Valley. The Tigers basically ran four plays in the game as they racked up 397 rushing yards on seventy carries.

Fuller closed out his Clemson career with a win over Ohio State in the Gator Bowl, concluding an 11-1 season and No. 6 final ranking for the Tigers. At the time, it was the highest final national ranking in school history.

The Spartanburg product was named the ACC Player of the Year for a second time that season and finished sixth in the Heisman Trophy race, the highest by a Clemson Tiger at the time. Fuller was an All-American on the football field as well as in the classroom, finishing Clemson with a perfect 4.0 GPA.

In his three seasons as the starting quarterback, Fuller guided the Tigers to a 22-9-3 record, including a 3-0 record against the Gamecocks. He left as the most decorated player in school history while joining Butler as first-round draft picks in the 1979 NFL draft. It was the first time that multiple Clemson players were selected in the first round of the draft. Butler went No. 5 to Buffalo, while Fuller was selected No. 23 overall by the Kansas City Chiefs.

II

A Crazy Start to Ford's Career

When Charley Pell met with his Clemson players earlier in the week, he told them that the news and rumors of him leaving Clemson to become the head coach at Florida were not true.

"He told us he was not going anywhere, and I think at the time he really believed he wasn't," All-American quarterback Steve Fuller recalled from that November afternoon in 1978.

Fuller also recalled that there was some discontent among the players due to the fact that Pell had accepted a bid to play in the Gator Bowl for a second straight year instead of waiting it out and possibly getting an Orange Bowl bid. Clemson accept its invitation to play Ohio State in the Gator Bowl following its win over Maryland, clinching the program's first ACC Championship in eleven years. "We did not blame Coach Pell for it completely, but he was the one that had to make that decision," Fuller said. "He made that decision and now he is going to go somewhere else to coach. That combination of things caused a little bit of uneasiness in our group."

Things got really uneasy later that afternoon, when Pell boarded a plane to Gainesville, Florida, where he later accepted the head-coaching job at the University of Florida. The next day, he called a team meeting at Clemson to tell his players of his departure. "I was like 'Wow!' I can remember going to Mulder Hall, which is where most of us lived. I can remember the meeting and he called everyone in on a Sunday night to tell everybody he was leaving," Fuller said. "We were not totally surprised, but we were more disappointed."

Prior to that meeting, Danny Ford, along with assistant coaches Tom Moore and Jimmye Laycock, had just got to Charlotte to scout the Shrine Bowl. The three Clemson assistants were checking into their hotel when they got a call from athletic director Bill McLellan telling them to return to Clemson immediately. "We got back in the car and went back home," Ford said. "We had no idea what was happening or why we were told to come back. No one had said anything. They said there was going to be a meeting and Coach Pell wanted everybody back in."

Ford said they speculated on the ride home what it might be, but they had no idea that Pell was going to leave Clemson. "He came into the meeting and told us he was going to Florida," said Ford. "That was kind of it. Then I met with the athletic director after the meeting and Pell was going to take four coaches and everybody else was going to be left on their own or maybe be retained at Clemson.

"After I heard all of that, it was a little surprising because I always felt that if they are good enough to coach with you here then they are good enough to coach with you there. That was always my opinion. I never had to do that, and I didn't know what he was facing. Was Florida telling him how many he could keep or if he had to keep others at Florida? All I know is there were four people going from our staff."

As for Clemson's upperclassmen, this was not a new thing for them. They were just two years removed from the last coaching change, so they knew how to compartmentalize what was happening. However, there was one thing that was different: they still had to play No. 20 Ohio State in the Gator Bowl.

"We had gone through the wars at that time and it was a pretty mature group," Fuller said. "We had a ton of senior leadership and it is a bowl game, too. It was not like we had five years of eligibility and were going to go through the whole coaching thing again."

Once Pell told the players he was moving on, Fuller and a few of the other seniors spoke with McLellan and suggested they should seriously consider Ford for the head-coaching job. "He was a part of it all and we liked him a lot and he's a dang good football coach," said Fuller.

McLellan ultimately did give Ford the job, and the plan was for Pell to coach the Tigers in the Gator Bowl. "In fact, he lobbied pretty hard. When he told us he was leaving, I think his words were, 'I'm going to Florida, but I will stay here and coach you guys through this thing,'" Fuller recalled.

But Clemson fans were not happy about what was happening. They felt Pell had lied to them and the players, and they were pretty vocal that they did not want him to coach the Tigers in the bowl game. They felt as if he was a deserter.

"Coach Pell held up the paper, the *Greenville News*, and said where he was not going to go and then it said 'Gator Bound' and had a big [headline] in the paper up there and I think that made a lot of Clemson people mad," Ford said. "They did not want him to coach [in the Gator Bowl] after they said he could coach. They made a commitment that he could coach, and until that picture came out in the paper, everything was fine."

One banner hanging from a building in downtown Clemson read, "Pell is a traitor." Soon after, bumper stickers started popping up in the Upstate that read, "To hell with Pell!"

"I think there was so much pressure from the athletic department, fans and everybody else. We were going to be down in Florida for two or three weeks practicing and getting ready for a football game that is played in Florida and Coach Pell would be basically down there recruiting for Florida. It did not sit too well with a lot of the Clemson people," said Fuller when thinking back to that time. "I think they kind of forced him out before he wanted to leave."

While the players were going to bat for Ford, the coaches who were not going with Pell to Florida had a staff meeting. Ford asked before the meeting if anyone wanted to apply for the job, because if they did, they needed to speak up and let everyone know. He wanted to get it all out in the open; he did not want any fighting among the staff. They still had a game to work together, and he wanted everything to be out in the open.

No one spoke up, though Ford thought defensive coordinator Mickey Andrews was a more qualified candidate than himself. Andrews had head coaching experience at Livingston and North Alabama, where he was before joining Pell's staff in 1977.

But Andrews, at least in the meeting, did not express any interest. When they asked Ford, "did he want to try to apply for the job," he said, "yes!"

"That was kind of it, and after that most of the players drafted a letter that Mike Brown took to Dr. Edwards," Ford said.

Brown, a trainer on the 1978 team, went on to law school and became an agent. In fact, he represented Dabo Swinney before his untimely death in January 2017. In all, seventy-five players signed the petition that Brown presented to Dr. Robert Edwards on behalf of the players to hire Ford as Clemson's next head coach.

"I think it was the work ethic he had shown. Obviously, he was a quality offensive line coach. Just his demeanor, his hardnose approach to everything. With Ford, there was no fluff to it at all. It was line up and bang heads and whoever the big and the strong was would come out of it," Fuller said. "I think he was the kind of guy we needed and felt like would keep it going. He was young and inexperienced for sure, similar to Dabo, but it felt right. Sometimes you make a decision and it works out."

Though McLellan did not publicly display any support for Pell staying on through the Gator Bowl, behind closed doors, he wanted Pell to stay. But the public outcry was too much, and it would cause tension and distraction inside the football program. "I was real disappointed when he left," said McLellan in *The Clemson Tigers: From 1896 to Glory*. "Emotions got into it with a lot of people, but it was a business decision. Charley was an awfully good organizer, a very intense person. He was a demanding taskmaster, and he started to achieve excellence here."

Years later, Ford received a copy of the players' petition to hire him. On December 5, 2017, thirty-nine years to the day he was named head coach at Clemson, Ford was inducted into the College Football Hall of Fame. For nearly forty years, Brown held on to that letter and carried it around in a labeled folder whenever he moved or changed jobs.

Brown was going to present it to Ford before he was enshrined, but he never got the opportunity. After his death, Brown's sisters came across the letter. It was in perfect condition. They had it framed and then presented it to Ford just weeks before his induction into the Hall of Fame.

"I have it at the house. To be a lawyer, he did not spell too well way back then," Ford joked. "As a lawyer and an agent, he needed to work on his spelling a little bit after I read it. But I had never seen it. I had heard about it, but I never saw it until they gave it to me two years ago at a ballgame at Clemson."

Ford admitted that he did not want to be the head coach in the Gator Bowl. "Personally, I did not want to start my career against Woody Hayes on national TV and had never been a head coach in a football game at all," he said. "I did not think it was a good idea and I did not think I was ready for it and basically, I was not ready for it.

"Luckily, we had good players that overcame my coaching. I was the offensive line coach and said whether we were going to receive or defend on the kickoff. Thank God, other than the fight, there were no major decisions to be made where you could lose the football game because of a stupid decision."

Ironically, it was Hayes who made the stupid decision. With Clemson ahead of the Buckeyes, 17–15, late in the fourth quarter, Ohio State was driving for what seemed like a potential winning score.

They were just about in field-goal range when quarterback Art Schlichter did not see defensive tackle Charlie Bauman drop into coverage. Schlichter threw the ball right to him, and the defensive tackle returned the interception up the Ohio State sideline, where he was tackled out of bounds.

As he got up to celebrate, Hayes grabbed Bauman and took a swing at the Clemson defender. Suddenly, a fracas broke out on the Buckeyes' sideline, involving Bauman, a few other Clemson players, the Buckeyes and Hayes. "We did not know what was happening," said Fuller, who was standing on the Clemson sideline. "We saw the play. Schlichter threw the ball right to Charlie. I don't think he ever saw him. Here is a nose tackle in the middle of a screen play, so I can see where that can happen. I have done that myself. But Charlie tries to run the ball and ends up on their sideline.

"It was a pile of humanity right there on their sideline. The referees were trying to figure out where the ball is and who has what. No one, with maybe the exception of Jim Stuckey, Charlie Bauman and a couple of guys that were right there, had any idea of what happened. We saw it on the news that night. I don't think Coach Ford knew. I think the media started asking him in the locker room. He did not know it. It was a very unusual situation."

In the hours leading up to the 1978 Gator Bowl, Danny Ford grew sick. He had no appetite as the game grew closer to kickoff. At thirty years old, Ford was the youngest head football coach in the country, and he wasn't sure he was ready to begin his career on such a big stage going against a legend and Hall of Fame coach such as Woody Hayes.

Though he was nervous, Ford's players did not know it. At the Gator Bow Luncheon, the day before the game, both teams, along with the media and fans, gathered together in a big ballroom at one of Jacksonville's fancy hotels. Hayes and Ford both addressed the audience.

"Coach Ford, in his modest way, stepped up first and says this is his first game and he is looking forward to the opportunity and he hopes Clemson represents the ACC and the university well, and we will play hard and do the best we can and thank you for having us," recalled Fuller. "Then they invite up Coach Hayes and literally, and I am not stretching this at all, he talks for 45 minutes and he is talking about Jack Nicklaus, John Havlicek and the great war heroes from Ohio State and the 1925 team. Coach Ford just stood up there, smiled and took it.

Former Clemson head coach Danny Ford speaks with reporters following the 1978 Gator Bowl against Ohio State. *Clemson Athletic Communications.*

"I think I was sitting next to Joe Bostic and said something like, 'If we ever needed some incentive to play hard, we are getting it right now.' He literally was up there acting like he was the President of the United States and we were fortunate enough to be able to play them. That was Coach Ford's first major and national exposure there and I think he came out of it on top."

Ford did not feel like he was on top. His stomach was torn up, and when the game was over, it took another several hours before he calmed down, especially with the way the game ended.

After getting back to the team hotel and celebrating a little with his players and coaches, Ford and his young wife, Deborah, went for a walk on Jacksonville's famous landing along the old St. Mary's River. "It was like two or three o'clock in the morning, and we needed something to eat. We were both starving to death," Ford said. "We found a little substation and got a sandwich before we walked back to the hotel."

When they got back to the hotel, all of the press was already there, and they started asking Ford his thoughts on Hayes being fired due to the punch he threw at Charlie Bauman. "We knew nothing about it and Charlie Bauman did a tremendous job not saying anything about it in the press and still to this day he will not talk about it," Ford said.

Ford said he does not remember much from the press conference later that morning except that, instead of it being about Clemson winning the game and he becoming the first coach to achieve his first win in a bowl game, all everyone wanted to do was talk about Hayes's punch and subsequent firing. Ford's first win as a head coach had already become old news.

Ford did not mind if he did not get the attention. He liked being in the background as much as he could. He always wanted to put his players and his program out in front.

12

The Year No One Could "Hold That Tiger"

It did not take long for Clemson to find itself back in the national spotlight, something it did frequently during the Danny Ford years. In 1981, the Tigers opened the season with wins over Wofford and Tulane when defending national champion Georgia came to Death Valley ranked No. 4 and owning the nation's longest winning streak.

Clemson forced a record nine turnovers that day and kept the Bulldogs out of the end zone in a 13–3 victory. The nine turnovers forced that afternoon is still a Clemson record. "I can remember when we played that if the offense lost the ball, we go tell them that we are going to get the ball back," said linebacker Jeff Davis, who led the Tigers in tackles and was an All-American in 1981. "I can remember that most of the time, that is exactly what happened."

Overall, the Tigers finished second nationally in scoring defense in 1981, seventh in rushing defense, seventh in turnover margin and eighth in total defense. Clemson led the ACC in total defense, rushing defense, scoring defense and interceptions. It forced a school record forty-one turnovers, which stands as the high mark in school history.

Clemson allowed just three teams to score more than 10 points in 1981—Wake Forest, South Carolina and Nebraska—and it went eighteen quarters without giving up a touchdown during one stretch. "We didn't want people to score on us, and we wanted to physically dominate people," Davis said. "In a sick way, that was our joy. Yeah, we may not have beaten everybody by 21 points, but your body and your mental state of mind said we beat you by

Clemson linebacker Jeff Davis prior to his final home game in a Clemson uniform in 1981. The Tigers beat Maryland that afternoon, 21–7, to win the program its eighth ACC Championship. *Clemson Athletic Communications.*

21 points. That's the kind of football we played. We had no reason for how great we were playing."

A player's coach, Ford knew what buttons to push to motivate individuals and his team. "He was a tough guy," Davis said. "He was very well respected. He had fire in him, and we fed off of that. He basically took what Charlie Pell started and took it to the next level. When we played for him it was hard for us to look ahead. It was hard for us to think too highly of ourselves because he had a way of pulling us back down."

Davis recalls that if it wasn't for Ford and his staff keeping the players grounded, especially after their win over Georgia, things might have been different in 1981. "The coaching staff did a good job of keeping us focused, keeping our goals out there and understanding that some great things can happen if we keep on playing the way we had been playing," he said. "I think that's why we won the national championship because we never really bought into the hype.

"We never bought into how great we were. It was more important for us to prove how great we were game in and game out."

With every passing week, critics from around the country predicted that this would be the week the Cinderella story from the small Upstate town in South Carolina would end. But each week, the Tigers found a way to win. When the offense finally got things going in the second half of its 21–3 victory over Kentucky, Clemson became a runaway train that ran over anything in its path. "It was about the business at hand," Davis said. "That is what our team focused on. It was the business at hand."

After the win over Kentucky, the Tigers steamrolled Virginia, 27–0. Then they scored 31 points in the second and third quarters in a 38–10 win at Duke. The offense then rushed for 304 yards in a 17–7 victory against NC State, before their record-setting 82–24 afternoon against Wake Forest on Halloween.

But the game that told the team, the coaching staff and the national media that 1981 was the year of the Clemson Tigers was its clash with North Carolina at Chapel Hill in Week 10.

Linebacker Jeff Davis makes a tackle on Georgia running back Herschel Walker in Clemson's 1981 win over the Bulldogs. *Clemson Athletic Communications.*

Clemson, 8-0, was ranked No. 2 by the Associated Press and No. 3 by United Press International (the Coaches Poll) coming into the November 7, 1981 game. The Tar Heels were 7-1 and ranked No. 8 in both major polls. "The North Carolina game did more for us winning the national championship than any other game," Davis said. "It was the ultimate test for us. We expected to win in Death Valley, and we expected teams to already be behind when the whistle blew in Death Valley. But, to go into the backyard of a top 10 football team with everything at stake, and win, that did it for us.

"Remember, North Carolina had everything to play for. It's right there for them. There were people wondering 'Can Clemson stay focused?' And we beat them in a fight. It was an all-out brawl. May the best man win! It was man-on-man."

This was the first time in the history of ACC football that two of its schools clashed in a battle of top 10 teams. With an ACC Championship and a major bowl bid at stake, it was dubbed the biggest game to ever be played in the state of North Carolina. "[North Carolina] came to play," defensive end Jeff Bryant said. "They were at home and they were a top 10 team. We both were striving for that goal which was to win the ACC and take it further from that. It was a very physical game. I can remember being sore for a couple of days after that."

It was also Homecoming Weekend in Chapel Hill and the last game at Kenan Stadium for UNC's seniors—a class that had helped the Tar Heels win an ACC Championship the year before and beat traditional powers such as Texas and Oklahoma along the way.

To top things off, there were representatives from eight bowl games in attendance, more than at any other game that afternoon across the country. *Sports Illustrated* had been at Clemson all week to chronicle the Tigers' magical run and was in Chapel Hill on that afternoon. ABC was broadcasting the game as part of its regional coverage and carried the game throughout most of the country.

With a victory over the No. 8 Tar Heels behind them, Clemson, for the first time, admitted that the possibility of going undefeated and playing for a national championship was on its mind. "It was important because we started thinking a little bit now about being undefeated," Davis said. "Until that point, we were not trying to touch it. There might have been a few rumblings here and there, but we were all about one game at a time.

"At that point, and where we were at, you were going to have to do something phenomenal to beat us."

Jeff Davis (*45*) and Andy Headen celebrate a fumble recovery in the Tigers' win over Nebraska in the 1982 Orange Bowl Classic. *Clemson Athletic Communications.*

The Tigers moved into the No. 1 spot for the first time in the program's history a week after they concluded the regular season with a win over rival South Carolina. Penn State beat Dan Marino and previously undefeated and No. 1 Pittsburgh, propelling Clemson to No. 1 in the rankings as it headed to play Nebraska in the Orange Bowl on New Year's Day.

The 1982 Orange Bowl was Clemson's first Orange Bowl appearance in twenty-five years. Homer Jordan, the game's Most Valuable Offensive Player, completed eleven of twenty-two passes and had 180 yards total offense in leading the Tigers, while Davis, the Defensive MVP of the game, had fourteen tackles. Bill Smith had a career high ten tackles to lead the linemen.

Clemson allowed just one pass completion in the second half as it went on to beat the fourth-ranked Cornhuskers, 22–15.

"We earned that thing," Davis said. "Not in a sense that we beat everybody or were more talented. We earned that thing on the practice field. That's where we won our national championship. We didn't win the national championship in the Orange Bowl in Miami. We won that thing on those practice fields. Coach Ford worked us. If I could say anything that could define us, I would say that was it. We knew how to work. When you know how to work, there is no give up and there is no satisfaction when you know how to work.

"The only thing you know is that I have to work until this last whistle and that's the mind-set," Davis continued. "Hard work equals mental toughness. Mental toughness means you do the little things. Doing the little things means that you are detailed and anything that is excellent is detailed.

"That thing has marked us for the rest of our lives. I know it has for me, anyway. No matter what it is, the car business, the ministry, the fundraising—I expect to be the best at what I do. That is how you know it is real."

13

IT ENDED WHERE IT STARTED

C lemson was as dominant of a program as there comes in the 1980s. The Tigers followed up the 1981 national championship with four more ACC Championships to go along with three more ten-win seasons. They finished ranked in the top 10 four other times and ranked inside the top 20 six more times.

Danny Ford led Clemson to wins over Hall of Fame coaches like Georgia's Vince Dooley, Nebraska's Tom Osborne, Penn State's Joe Paterno and Oklahoma's Barry Switzer. The Tigers appeared in six bowl games in the decade, winning five of them.

The Tigers went 87-25-4 in the 1980s, the fifth-best record of the decade in all of college football.

"We had a lot of good teams and a couple of really good teams," Ford said. "We never could quite duplicate what we did in 1981. We came close a couple of times, but it's hard to win every game. You got to catch a few breaks here and there, but we had some really good football teams."

Clemson's success in the late 1970s and the 1980s did not come without some controversy, though.

At the end of the 1982 season, an NCAA investigation found some wrongdoings within the football program regarding recruiting that dated back to 1977. The NCAA, along with the ACC, placed Clemson on probation for the 1983 and 1984 seasons. The program could not appear on national or regional television during that period. It was also ineligible for any conference championship and postseason bowl games.

Clemson players carry Danny Ford off the Orange Bowl playing field following the Tigers' 22–15 win over Nebraska to clinch the 1981 national championship. *Clemson Athletic Communications.*

In hopes to get ahead of the NCAA sanctions, Clemson University president Dr. William Atchley announced before the conclusion of the 1982 season that the school would not participate in any bowl game as a self-proposed punishment. The program was in the running for a Cotton Bowl appearance, closing the 1982 season with nine straight wins and securing a second consecutive ACC Championship.

Clemson again went 9-1-1 in 1983, winning its last eight games to close out the season. In 1984, the weight of probation began to show, as the Tigers slipped to 7-4. Things were supposed to get back to normal in 1985, but the football program came under scrutiny again when a former student assistant strength coach, who worked for the athletic department, told the *Greenville News* that he had provided five football players with steroids during the 1984 season.

Ford was angry that the *Greenville News* ran such a piece and denied that he or anyone on his coaching staff knew anything about it. Ford released a statement in response to the article, publicly stating that the football program had nothing to do with the claims written in the *Greenville News.*

This was happening during a time when the athletic department was under attack after two track coaches were investigated by the South Carolina Law Enforcement Division for illegally dispensing prescription drugs to student athletes. Both coaches eventually resigned. But the damage was done.

With another black cloud cast above the football program as it was coming off probation—and the issues with the track team—Atchley had seen enough. A power struggle for control of the athletic department began between he and athletic director Bill McLellan.

In the end, both men were out. Atchley resigned after the board of trustees decided they were going to remove Atchley as university president. Ultimately, he resigned after the board refused to honor his request for a vote of confidence. As for McLellan, he was forced to retire in late July, just as football practice was about to begin. The retirement of McLellan was in large for the good of the university, as it hoped to repair the damage from Atchley's and McLellan's feud.

Bobby Robinson was named as McLellan's replacement as athletic director, and the school tried to move forward. However, late in the season, in a critical game against Maryland, as the Tigers tried to earn a bowl bid in their first year back from probation, the reputation of the football program took another hit. After a couple of calls did not go Clemson's way in a 34–31 loss, Ford stormed the field and had a colorful conversation with the game's officials. Ford expressed his displeasures and, unfortunately for he and Clemson, CBS's microphones picked up every word Ford said.

Things only got worse, Maryland defensive back Lewis Askew, who had tackled Clemson return man Terrance Roulhac out of bounds near the Tigers' sideline on the ensuing kick, was punched by several Clemson players as they walked by. CBS caught the acts on camera.

It was another public-relations mess for Clemson's athletic department. Ultimately, Ford and six of his players were disciplined by the university and the ACC. For his actions, Ford was put on one-year probation and was suspended from the sideline for the 1986 game at Maryland. The six players were suspended for the South Carolina game.

Clemson rallied to beat the Gamecocks in Columbia that next Saturday and afterward accepted a bid to play Minnesota in the Independence Bowl in Shreveport, Louisiana. The Tigers lost the game and finished the year a mediocre 6-6, the worst record under Ford in his eleven seasons as Clemson's head coach.

In June 1986, the Clemson football program was again under scrutiny when star tailback Kenny Flowers, a Heisman Trophy candidate, and one of his teammates, A.J. Johnson, as well as two former Clemson players, were accused of sexual assault, kidnapping and robbery. Ultimately, eleven days before Clemson's season opener against Virginia Tech, all four men were cleared by a Pickens Country grand jury.

For the next three years, things quieted down in regard to the football program. Clemson got back to the top of the ACC by winning three consecutive conference crowns in 1986, '87 and '88. However, after Clemson completed a 10-2 season in 1989—the program's third straight 10-win season—the wrongdoings discovered in another NCAA investigation were revealed and did not look good. In all, the NCAA alleged that the Clemson football program committed thirty-seven violations from 1984 to 1988. It was another black cloud above the school's athletic department.

This time, Ford could not survive it. Coincidently, Ford's last game as Clemson's head coach happened to be in the same place where he had first coached the Tigers in a win at the Gator Bowl in Jacksonville.

Ford ultimately resigned, though Robinson would not confirm that the NCAA's findings had anything to do with Ford being pushed out. Some

Danny Ford and former Clemson linebacker Terrence Mack. *Clemson Athletic Communications.*

believe it was the rift between Ford and university president Max Lennon. Ford wanted a new dorm for his players, while Lennon wanted to build an academic-enrichment facility on campus for all student athletes.

In the summer of 1989, Bob Cole, a writer for *The State*, attended an IPTAY meeting in Columbia. "Coach Ford basically got up there and said, 'We don't need an academic center. We need an athletic dorm so we can keep up with recruiting,'" longtime Clemson sports information director Tim Bourret recalled. "Well, that did not go over very well with the academic side of things. Obviously, that made it worse across the campus.

"There were a lot of things that kind of contributed to it," Bourret said.

On January 17, 1990, Ford was notified in a letter from Robinson that he was no longer the head coach at Clemson. Later that night, Ford called his coaches off the road from recruiting and told them to return to Clemson.

At 8:00 a.m. the next morning, Ford told his staff that he was resigning. At 11:30 a.m., he addressed his team and said he was resigning for the betterment of the university. Robinson told reporters that Ford's resignation was the result of basic philosophical differences and honest differences of opinion on certain aspects of the program. In a press release issued by the university, Ford denied any wrongdoing and said he was confident that he would be exonerated at the conclusion of the NCAA's investigation.

On January 21, 1990, an angry crowd gathered outside the President's Box at Memorial Stadium as the university was set to name Ken Hatfield its next head coach. In the four days since Ford had stepped down, fans, alumni and even players expressed their displeasure at his departure. "That morning, I met with security, and keep in mind, things were so crazy, and the fans were upset," Bourret said. "I will never forget this. So, I am meeting with the security people and we are going over all the logistics for the press conference, which we had not even announced we were going to have.

"This meeting was around nine o'clock, so I go in there and the police want to know and say, 'Tim, where do you think we can put the security in case the fans storm the President's Box during the press conference?'

"That's how serious it was. I thought to myself, 'Oh my God! What did I get myself into?' Remember, this was my first year being in charge."

Hatfield handled the situation with class and poise, and he got a little help from a Hall of Fame coach. "Thank God for Coach [Frank] Howard that day," Bourret recalled. "There were a lot of people outside that day at the bottom of the hill on that Sunday. Coach Howard went out there before Coach Hatfield got there and he kind of calmed everybody down. And said,

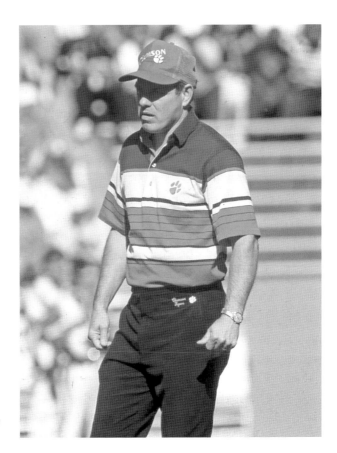

Ken Hatfield coached at Clemson from 1990 to 1993 while producing a 32-13-1 record and winning an ACC Championship in 1991. *Clemson Athletic Communications.*

'I like Coach Ford, but I first pull for Clemson and I am going to support who the coach is, and you should, too.' It was something like that and he did calm them down."

After Howard talked to the angry mob, he came in and asked Hatfield if he would come out and say a few words. Hatfield was happy to. With his wife, Sandy, Hatfield, a man of strong Christian values and faith, walked through the crowd until he was in the middle of them all. "I'm glad you are here," he told the group. "That shows people at Clemson really care. It shows interest, enthusiasm and your concern for this purpose. I'm not going to ask you or force you to accept me right away. I have to prove myself."

While the new Clemson coach seemed to be calming down the fans, he had a different problem inside the locker room. Four days earlier, when Ford called a team meeting, it caught all the players off guard. "Everyone was like, 'Why are we having a team meeting,'" linebacker and 1989 Gator Bowl

MVP Levon Kirkland said. "'What's up? What's going on?' You could feel that something was wrong."

Ford gathered the team and told them he and the university reached a boiling point and had reached an impasse they could not get around. The end result was his resignation. "You could have heard a pin drop," Kirkland recalled. "You could see that some guys took it better than others, but collectively, we were very upset."

They were so upset that members of the team joined fans and students and marched over to Lennon's house the next night. This was on Friday, January 19, 1990. The team threatened to boycott the 1990 football season if Ford was not reinstated.

Defensive end Vance Hammond and running back Stacey Fields represented the players when they spoke to the media. "They had a march from Tillman Hall to the president's home, and I mean with a lot of people," Bourret said. "Max Lennon had smartly heard of this and he and his wife went somewhere else. They stayed somewhere else, so nobody ever came to the door. But there were a lot of people yelling and screaming outside of his house."

Lennon was actually with Robinson and another Clemson administrator in Memphis interviewing Hatfield.

"I think you have to understand that we were a team that just came off a big victory against West Virginia in the Gator Bowl and I think everybody's feelings coming back that year was that we had an opportunity to go all the way and bid for a national championship," said Kirkland. "Now, we were young men. You have to realize that we weren't fully matured. When you have someone that everybody looked up to, that was tough.

"The coaches' and players' relationships seemed to really mesh at the time. The players seemed to really enjoy the coaches and the coaches seemed to have really enjoyed the players. We worked hard and it seemed like it was a great understanding. To break it up was tough. There was not a whole lot we could really, really do, but we thought being a team; we thought we could maybe sway the decision."

Eventually, the players on the team, especially leaders like Kirkland, middle guard Rob Bodine and quarterback DeChane Cameron, took ownership and brought an understanding to the team that Ford wasn't coming back and that they had to rally behind their new head coach. They called for a players-only meeting to discuss their futures and how they were going to handle things from here on out.

"I was one of those guys who said, 'Hey let's give this guy a chance,'" said Kirkland, who went on to play eleven years in the NFL, including nine with the Pittsburgh Steelers. "'I want to continue to play. I think I have a future at it. I'm not willing to throw that away.' Plus, I come from a family that's a humble family. We just didn't have the money to try and do that.

"I didn't want to do all that changing. I think a lot of guys realized that, too. We just did not want to throw this away. Coach Hatfield was a good coach. He was a very good man and we had to give it a try."

14

SPILLER ALWAYS KNEW DABO WAS THE RIGHT MAN FOR THE JOB

There was not much noise. Everyone was quiet and lost in their thoughts, including running back C.J. Spiller.

Just a few hours earlier, back in Winston-Salem, North Carolina, he and his Clemson teammates had suffered one of their most embarrassing losses of their college careers. Wake Forest—undermanned and nowhere near as talented as a Tigers team that started the season ranked No. 9 in the country and the media's pick to win the Atlantic Coast Conference for the first time in seventeen years—beat them, 12–7, on a Thursday night at Groves Stadium.

"For me it sucked because I got hurt during that game," Spiller recalled. "So, I was beating myself up about that situation, and then you lose on top of that and the way that we lost. Everything that could possibly go wrong in that game, it went wrong."

The Tigers rolled into Clemson in the early-morning hours of October 10, 2008. What was once thought to be a promising season now saw the team at 3-3 and 1-2 in the ACC. What happened in the days to come, no one on the team saw coming. "I think our mindset was, 'What could we do to turn this season around and get it back on track,'" Spiller said.

Athletic Director Terry Don Phillips and the Clemson administration had the same mind-set, except they wanted to do it with a different guy in charge. After being embarrassed by Alabama on national television in the season opener, plus blowing a 17-point lead at home to Maryland in a 20–17 loss the Saturday before going to Winston-Salem, rumors had already started to circulate about Tommy Bowden's demise as head coach.

As for the team, no one was talking about it. Spiller had no idea the rumors were going around. "I think if guys would have known that, it kind of would have put more pressure on us," Spiller said. "I have said this many times, I don't think we had the teams built for how to handle success and how to handle disappointment.

"I don't think no one in the locker room knew what was about to happen."

The Tigers had the weekend off and returned to practice Sunday evening. After practice was over, Bowden told the media that Willy Korn was the team's new starting quarterback for the upcoming game against Georgia Tech, hoping the move could jump-start his team and perhaps save his job. Bowden had no idea that this was the last time he would speak to the media as Clemson's head coach.

Phillips arrived on campus a little bit earlier than he normally did on October 13, 2008. He knew Bowden was an early riser and was always in his office at the McFadden Building before 7:00 a.m. Phillips felt it was best that he spoke with Bowden before everyone else in the athletic department rolled into work.

He was very upfront with his football coach, telling him that unless they found a way to turn things around and win the ACC's Atlantic Division, the school would replace him at season's end. Phillips then walked back across the breezeway to his office in the Jervey Athletic Center. What happened next caught him and everyone else off guard.

After some time had passed, Bowden walked into Phillips's office and offered him a deal. He would step away as head coach immediately as long as Phillips agreed to make Dabo Swinney the interim head coach. Bowden, as he still does, thought the world of his young wide receivers coach. He knew Swinney was head-coaching material and wanted to see him have a shot. Phillips felt the same way, as Swinney had caught his attention long before by the way he carried himself, coached his players, recruited and was so beloved by many of the players on the team.

Spiller does not remember exactly where he was on that Monday morning when he found out Bowden had resigned and Swinney, the guy responsible for him being at Clemson, was named the interim. He knows that he was either in class or over at Vickery Hall, the old academic services building, when he started receiving text messages from friends, family and teammates about the news. "Of course, we were in there with other students and they were on the internet and stuff like that and we were like, 'Man! What just happened,'" Spiller said.

As he headed to the team meeting that afternoon, Spiller had one hundred thoughts going through his mind. There was the disappointment of the

Dabo Swinney points to the heavens prior to running down the hill for the first time as Clemson's interim head coach in 2008. *Clemson Athletic Communications.*

season to think about, his head coach was no longer there and they had to play Georgia Tech in five days. Plus, he knew he was likely not going to play due to a hamstring injury he had suffered at Wake Forest.

Spiller remembers vividly what happened next. In the team meeting, Swinney asked all the coaches to leave the room so that he could talk to the team by himself. In the next thirty or so minutes, the foundation of the Clemson culture everyone knows today was first laid down. Swinney was upfront with the players. He told them what Phillips had relayed to him. He said he was not just the interim coach who would merely manage the program until someone else came along, but he was the head coach. If they were able to turn the season around, he would have an opportunity to interview for the job and could possibly get it.

At that moment, Swinney told the players that if anyone wanted to leave right then and there, he understood. They could keep their scholarship and, when the new coach was named, could come back to the team. But if they decided to step foot on the practice field that night, they had to be "all in" and do everything they could to help turn things around. There was no in-between. They had to either have both feet in or both feet out. The choice was theirs, and no one was going to think differently about them either way. "The room was very quiet," Spiller recalled. "You could hear a pin drop in there. Guys were still trying to process what happened with Coach Bowden. Everybody knew Coach Swinney and what type of person he is and what type of coach he is, just from looking at how he coached his guys.

"Now he is the leader of the team and he was very up-front with us. I think that is why everyone showed up to that Monday night practice. When he told us, 'Your scholarship will be honored if you don't want to be here, but if you come to practice tonight, just know that you have to be all in, and we have nothing to lose.'"

Swinney immediately began to put his stamp on the program. Knowing he needed to bring the fan base and the team back together, he incorporated Tiger Walk for the very first time that following Saturday. Instead of the team being dropped off right in front of the locker room as they had done forever, he instead had the players dropped off at Perimeter Road, right in front of Lot 5 and had them walk through a sea of Clemson fans who he knew would love and support them no matter what.

"It was crazy," Spiller remembers about the first Tiger Walk. "It was nuts to see so many people show up. It was a twelve o'clock game, if I am not mistaken, and to see so many fans show up for that was awesome. No one knew what to expect. The fans did not know. The players, we didn't know.

"Coach said we are going to do this Tiger Walk and he knew the fans would show up and greet us as we walked into the stadium. As we pulled up and saw so many fans before the game cheering for us, it gave us energy. It gave us some life."

Though they played tough and gave it their all, in spite of all that had transpired just five days before, Clemson lost that first game under Swinney, 21–17, to Georgia Tech. However, Spiller could see things had changed and that they believed they could turn the season around.

They had an open date the following week prior to playing at Boston College. They all knew this was the game that was going to make or break their season. A win at BC would give them the opportunity they needed to become bowl eligible. "We wanted to get to a bowl game, and we wanted to give the seniors the opportunity to play just one last game," Spiller said. "We knew we had to start stacking some wins together. Boston College was the next opponent and we knew it was going to be a tough game."

Since it joined the ACC in 2005, Boston College had not lost to Clemson, winning three straight thrillers over the Tigers. The 2008 game was no different. Clemson jumped out to a 17–0 halftime lead behind the running of Spiller and his backfield teammate James Davis. Cullen Harper had won back the starting quarterback job, and the offense was finally clicking again.

However, Spiller, who had 242 total yards, had to leave the game in the third quarter with a head injury following a 40-yard catch-and-run and BC came roaring back. The Eagles scored 21 unanswered points to take a 21–17 lead with 8:43 to play in the game.

But Spiller was cleared by the medical staff at Clemson and returned the ensuing kickoff 64 yards to set up what turned out to be the game-winner, a 3-yard touchdown pass from Harper to Aaron Kelly that was first ruled out of bounds but was overturned by replay officials.

The Tigers went on to win the game, 27–21. It was Swinney's first victory as a head coach. "We had been through so much so to finally get that win, there was just so much emotion," Spiller said. "You would have thought we won the national championship. Everyone was just so excited. There were guys jumping up and down, guys crying and hugging each other because we knew we finally got that monkey off our back."

It had been almost five weeks since Clemson had last won a game. Now, with new life breathed back into the program, the players believed in Swinney and knew things were on the upswing.

After playing Florida State tough down in Tallahassee the following week, the Tigers returned home and routed Duke, 31–7, before beating Virginia,

Dabo Swinney and former running back C.J. Spiller embrace following the Tigers' win at Boston College in 2008. It was Swinney's first win as a head coach. *Clemson Athletic Communications.*

13–3, the following week in Charlottesville. That set up a showdown with archrival South Carolina at Death Valley in the regular-season finale.

At 6-5, because it had beat Football Championship Sub-division foe South Carolina State earlier in the year, Clemson had to beat the Gamecocks to become bowl eligible. However, going to a bowl game and having bragging rights was not the only thing up in the air. Swinney learned earlier in the week that if he beat Steve Spurrier and his Gamecocks in the finale, the Clemson job was his. "We did not know that as players," Spiller said. "I don't think it would have changed the way that we would have played, though. We knew the magnitude of the game. But it would have added some extra juice to it."

"We kind of had a sense in the locker room that if we win this one, there might be a possibility of Coach getting this job, but he never came out and said it. He has never been about that. He always wants us to play our best football. He understands the magnitude of this game. He wanted to make sure our fans had the opportunity to have bragging rights and that is how we looked at it. We also wanted to do it for our seniors because this was their last game in Death Valley."

The Gamecocks never had a chance. Playing for the seniors, the fans and, ultimately, Swinney, Clemson jumped out to a 24–0 lead thanks to two Davis touchdowns and Jacoby Ford's 50-yard touchdown reception from Cullen Harper on a trick play called "Cock-a-doodle-doo."

As the final minutes and seconds started to wind down in Clemson's 31–14 victory, the eighty-two thousand fans packed into Memorial Stadium began to chant "DABO SWINNEY! DABO SWINNEY!" over and over again.

"We knew then he got the job," Spiller said. "Once you win the fans over, it is like a done deal here. Once we got those chants going and we carried him off the field, we knew he got the job."

Swinney was officially named the head coach two days later.

"I just remember sitting there in that press conference knowing we have the right person to lead our program," Spiller said. "I knew it was going to take time to get the right pieces that he needed. It was the first time he was the head coach, so he was figuring out the ins and outs of what that all meant, but I knew he was the right person."

And now, ten years and two national championship later, everyone else does, too.

15

DIVINE INTERVENTION?

It was just like any other summer practice in the month of August.

It was hot. It was humid. For Terry Don Phillips, it was life as usual.

For more years than he can count, Phillips, a former football coach, spent his afternoons in August watching football practice. "It is just something I have always enjoyed doing," he said. Phillips liked to go out and observe. He liked to watch the different styles of coaching, see how a coach tried to teach his players the game he grew up playing and coaching for so many years.

Though he was the athletic director at Clemson University, Phillips was a football coach first. His passion for teaching young people the game he loves so much never changed, even when he got into the administrative side of things. "I just like to go out there and watch. I liked to see how coaches teach. I liked to see how they motivate their players. I enjoyed seeing the players develop and progress through coaching."

However, on a particular August afternoon in 2003, Phillips came across a young coach he suddenly became fascinated by. It was not abnormal to see a coach fussing at his players. That usually comes with the territory. But this time, it was different.

"I usually will go and watch the defense," Phillips said. "I like to watch how they are coaching and how they are doing things. I generally will stay over there. I would look at the offense, but I generally would stay on the defensive side."

On this particular day, Phillips found himself intrigued by Clemson's new wide receivers coach. "All I heard was this loud and intense voice on that side

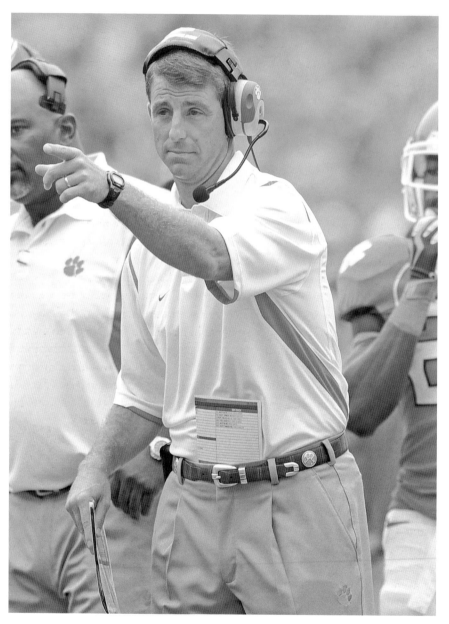

Dabo Swinney walking the sidelines early in his career as head coach. *Clemson Athletic Communications.*

of the field. He was getting after them. But he was not yelling at them. He was coaching them. He was coaching them intently. I could tell that he was passionate about what he was teaching them. I wanted to see more."

More and more during the course of camp, Phillips saw Dabo Swinney coaching up his players.

"It was not so much that he was coaching them as much as he was teaching them," Phillips added. "He fussed at them and he got on them pretty good, but it's the way he did it that was so intriguing. As soon as practice was over, he was loving on them and making sure they understood how much he cared about them.

"He does that better than anyone I have ever seen."

For the next five years, Phillips kept his eye on the young coach from Pelham, Alabama. He noticed in the football offices how the players all seem to migrate to him, and not just his position players, but even defensive players.

Swinney recruited a lot of the players that played for Tommy Bowden in those days, but not all of them. Yet, every time Phillips walked across the breezeway from the Jervey Athletic Center to the McFadden Building, he always noticed how Swinney had players in his office. "He had such a great relationship with those kids, they would run through a brick wall for him," Phillips said. "When I would walk through McFadden, he would always have kids in his office, and they were not necessarily his position players. The kids migrated to him. That in and of itself is an extremely important barometer with regard with that relationship you have with student athletes."

Though he did not know of Swinney's desire to be a head coach, Phillips saw a potential head coach in Dabo Swinney, and if the opportunity ever presented itself, he would give him a chance.

But that opportunity almost did not happen. Following the 2006 season, Swinney came into Phillips's office and asked for a favor. "Of course, Dabo wanted to be a head coach," Phillips said. "It wasn't that he wanted to leave the program or anything, but he was like every other young coach. He wanted to be a head coach. If he had an opportunity to go somewhere and prove himself, he would have liked to have done that."

Swinney handed Phillips his résumé and asked if he might put in a good word. He had applied to be the head coach at South Alabama, which was just starting its program. "I would not have taken the job if it was offered," Swinney said, "but I needed to go through the process. I needed to know what it was like. I put a lot of time and energy into it. I pursued it as if it was my dream job."

However, South Alabama was not the only job Swinney applied for. There was another. The University of Alabama–Birmingham job opened up, and in Phillips's mind, Swinney seemed like a perfect fit. "Dabo gave me his résumé and everything and I tried my best to talk to them about Dabo, but I could not get to first base with them, which we were very fortunate that occurred," Phillips said.

But Clemson was not out of the woods just yet. At the same time, Alabama started courting Swinney to be its new passing-game coordinator.

The Crimson Tide was set to hire Rich Rodriguez to be its new head coach. Swinney was actually going to go coach at Alabama, again, and the night before Rodriguez was to tell his West Virginia team he was leaving to take the job at Alabama, the story was leaked to ESPN.

"Once it got leaked out, he got nervous and backed out," Swinney said. "The only reason I know this is because Mal Moore was keeping me in the loop. Rich Rod decided to stay at West Virginia and Mal was back to square one."

Moore then proceeded to go after Nick Saban, again. Saban, who was the Miami Dolphins head coach at the time, had already said no to Moore. But this time, the Alabama athletic director did not take no for an answer. He convinced Saban to leave Miami for 'Bama.

The Clemson running backs coach at the time, Burton Burns, left the school to join Saban's staff, and he tried to convince Swinney to join him in Tuscaloosa. Saban offered Swinney a lucrative deal to be his passing-game coordinator. "It was a lot of money, but it was bad timing," Swinney said. "It just did not feel right. My spirit was not feeling good about it."

One reason was that Swinney was loyal to Bowden. The former Clemson head coach took a chance on him after Swinney had been out of coaching for two years when others would not. That meant something to Swinney. "Tommy Bowden deserves a lot of credit. He had the guts to hire me. I had been out of coaching for two years and I had a lot of doors closed on me. But Coach Bowden believed in me and he gave me an opportunity."

Swinney was also loyal to the recruits he was about to sign and to his players. "It was bad timing. I had six guys committed and I did not want to do that to them. Coach Bowden had been good to me, and I did not want to leave him hanging. At the time, I did not know Nick. I knew nothing about him.

"It just did not feel right. I did not have a good spirit about it."

However, Swinney did use the Alabama courtship as some leverage. At the time, he, like a lot of the coaches on the Clemson staff, was on a one-year contract. But Swinney wanted a two-year deal for a little more job security. "I met with Terry Don, and he did not blink an eye, so I stayed on." Clemson dodged a bullet. At the time, they had no idea how big the bullet was.

Bowden stepped aside on October 13, 2008, and gave Swinney an opportunity to show what he could do. What he did was become the first interim coach to take over a team at midseason and guide that team to a bowl game. He was the first interim coach in the history of college football to finish the year with a winning record.

Following a 31–14 victory over archrival South Carolina to close the regular season, Phillips hired Swinney as the next head coach. "If I had not had the opportunity to be the interim, I'm probably not here," Swinney said.

Phillips gave Swinney complete autonomy. For seven weeks, he could run the program the way he would run it if it was his own. "This was an opportunity to see how he would do," Phillips said.

"I walked out of his office walking on the clouds," Swinney said. "I was empowered and energized because of his belief in me."

Swinney thrived, primarily due to the five-minute conversation he had with Phillips. Clemson proceeded to beat Boston College, Duke, Virginia and South Carolina to close the regular season with four wins in its final five games. A lot of people were surprised by the Tigers' strong finish with an interim coach at the helm. Not Phillips.

"He was happy to see me get an opportunity, but we both knew I was going to have to win some games to have a chance," Swinney said. "We were able to get it going. So, it kind of made it easy for him. He told me up front, 'I would love to see you get this job. I think you are ready for this job. I think you would be a great fit. You are just going to have to find some way to win some games. I want you to be the head coach. I don't want you to be the interim head coach. I want you to act like the head coach, think like the head coach and do whatever you need to do to fix this. Whatever it is, I'm going to support you and let's go for the next seven weeks. You will get an interview no matter what.'

"The fact that we were able to win some games made it easier, but he took a huge chance. He knew he was going to be tied directly to that decision."

Phillips did not care. He saw something in Swinney no one else did. "Our program is not where it is without Terry Don," Swinney said. "He went with his gut and with his instinct. He watched me for five and a half years. He knew what I could do.

"There are very few athletic directors out there that would have given me that opportunity."

Dabo Swinney is carried off the field after beating rival South Carolina, 31–14, in 2008. Swinney was named the Tigers' permanent head coach the following Monday. *Clemson Athletic Communications.*

On December 1, 2008, the interim tag was removed from Swinney's title. He was now the head coach of the Clemson Tigers.

"Terry Don told me when he hired me, 'You just continue to be who you are. Go with your gut and your instincts and I'm going to support you,'" Swinney said. "'We are in this for the long haul. I believe in you. I think you are going to be one of the best coaches in the country. But there will be some good times and some bad times, but I just want you to know that I got your back.

"'I don't want you to be distracted by things that don't matter. If it doesn't work, I will help you pack, and you can help me pack and we will go together.'"

That nearly happened in 2010. Injuries and a lack of depth derailed the Tigers. The season concluded with four losses in their last six games. But there was a sign of promise. Clemson lost five of its seven games by six points or less and another one by just nine points.

The only game in which they did not have a chance to win was against the Gamecocks, who beat the Tigers, 29–7. It marked the first time South Carolina defeated Clemson in back-to-back years since the 1968–'70 era.

"That was a low point. Everybody felt awful," Phillips said. "But when things are going great, everyone is doing great, but to really get a true evaluation of a person is to see how they handle things when things are not going well."

Phillips said Swinney was never changed. In spite of everything that was going on outside of the football program's office that year, what the media and those on social media were saying, his young coach never changed his approach. He stayed strong. He stayed consistent for his coaches and his staff.

As he walked through the hall on the second floor of the West Zone of Memorial Stadium following the loss to South Carolina, a dejected Swinney saw his wife coming down the hall to tell him that Phillips was in his office. "I was like, 'Well, it was a nice two-year run,'" Swinney said.

Swinney wasn't sure what to expect when he walked into his office. The room was dark with the exception of one light, and sitting on the couch in the shadows was Phillips. "What was in my mind, my mind was totally opposite of what I got," Swinney said.

Swinney knew Phillips had a lot of pressure on him as well. "Terry Don looked at me and said, 'Dabo let me tell you something. I know it's a tough time and there is going to be some negativity, there is going to be some criticism and there is going to be this and that,'" Swinney recalled. "'But here is what I want you to know. I'm more confident right now, at this moment that you are the guy for this job and that you will be successful than I was before I hired you. That's all I have to say.'"

Phillips's objective that night was to make sure Swinney knew he had his total support. He did not want his young head coach to think that any of the things people were saying were true. "I felt stronger about him than when I hired him," Phillips said. "That was a tough year. People were all around our necks.

"The way he handled adversity. The way he handled his staff. How he handled the players and how he handled himself publicly, tells you more about the kind of person they are than when everything is going well. It is easy to do those things when everything is going good."

It started to get easy for Phillips and Swinney in 2011. Thanks to talented players like Tajh Boyd, Dwayne Allen, Deandre Hopkins and a superstar freshman by the name of Sammy Watkins, Clemson rose to the top of the ACC for the first time in twenty years. They also won ten games in a season for the first time in twenty-one years. "I knew he could get the job done," Phillips said. "I did not want to have any regrets. I knew he was going to be great, and darn it, I did not want him to be great somewhere else."

Swinney has become the greatest coach in Clemson history and one of the best in the country. The Tigers won their second national title in three years with its 44–16 win over Alabama in the 2019 College Football Playoff National Championship Game.

For more than three decades, Clemson fans longed for another 1981 season, another national championship. Swinney has delivered two, including a 15-0 season—the first in the modern era of college football. "We rolled the dice when we hired Dabo. He did not have the pedigree," Phillips said. "But I just felt like Dabo had some special characteristics in regard to how he treated players, how he felt about players and you could see why he was successful in attracting good quality young people to come into the program. When you step back, you say, 'I think this is worth the gamble.'

"I did not really feel like it was a gamble because I believed in due time that it would work out. Certainly, in those early years there were people all over me and they were not being very kind."

In the eleven years Swinney has been at the helm at Clemson, the Tigers have not only won two national championships, but they are also 130-31. They won six ACC Championships, including the last five. They have won ten bowl games, beating college football powerhouses such as Alabama, Oklahoma and Ohio State on multiple occasions, as well as LSU and Notre Dame.

Besides Alabama, Clemson is the only program in the country with nine consecutive ten-win seasons and joins Alabama and Ohio State as the only schools with one hundred or more wins this past decade.

"God orders your steps when you are seeking Him," Swinney said. "This is what He wanted for me. I had every worldly reason to take that job with Alabama back in 2006. I was going to take it if Rich Rod took the job. But, that's not what God wanted me to do.

"I don't know why, but I just could not do that to Coach Bowden or to Clemson. It is weird how it all worked out."

It is hard to imagine what Clemson might be like if Swinney had been offered the UAB job or took the job with Saban at Alabama. "I truly believe the Good Lord is looking after Dabo because a lot of these things just sort of fall into place," Phillips said.

16

B.Y.O.G.

It had been thirty-eight years since the "Golden Domers" last visited Clemson's Death Valley. On that day, a guy named Joe Montana rallied No. 5 Notre Dame from ten points down in the fourth quarter to break No. 15 Clemson's heart.

Few expected the same kind of ending when the Irish brought a freshman quarterback named DeShawn Kizer into Death Valley on October 3, 2015, for a prime-time game that was being seen nationally on ABC. Kizer, barley wet between the ears as a college quarterback, was no Joe Montana. He was not even the starting quarterback when the season began. That honor belonged to Malik Zaire. But when Zaire broke his foot in the fourth quarter at Virginia, Kizer was thrown into action. He did have a Montana-like moment in that game, when he threw a 39-yard touchdown pass to wide receiver Will Fuller with twelve seconds to play to beat the Cavaliers.

But No. 11 Clemson was not Virginia. If the Tigers were able to get out to a two-score lead on the Irish in the second half this time around, there would be no miraculous comeback.

Kizer played well in beating Georgia Tech and UMass the two weeks before the journey to Clemson. He was completing 67.7 percent of his passes for 541 yards and five touchdowns to go against two interceptions.

But Clemson was his first game on the road as the starter. It's Death Valley. There are 85,000 people screaming at him, not for him. How would he handle it? If Clemson could take away the running game, which was defensive coordinator Brent Venables's game plan, could the freshman make

Deshaun Watson played a big role in the Tigers' 24–22 victory over Notre Dame in 2015. *The Clemson Insider.*

the necessary plays to beat the Tigers when he had to throw the ball in obvious passing situations?

As for Clemson and quarterback Deshaun Watson, they were looking for respect. Heading into their clash with No. 6 Notre Dame, all they heard was how great the Irish were and how Clemson would not be able to match their physicality on either side of the ball.

In a way, he felt like Clemson was getting disrespected or not getting the credit it deserved for beating teams like Oklahoma, Ohio State and LSU in the previous three seasons. "From what I have been seeing we have kind of never had that respect, and for some reason we can't get over that hump," Watson said.

There was a reason why the media and the so-called experts were thinking Clemson could not beat the Irish. In the first two weeks, Clemson took out FCS foe Wofford, 49–10, and then beat App State, 41–10. Not exactly powerhouses. Then the Tigers struggled at Louisville in Week 3, escaping with a 20–17 victory to open up the ACC season.

In each of the previous two weeks, Clemson had fallen in the polls despite the fact that it had not lost a game. After beating Louisville, the Tigers dropped from No. 9 in the Amway Coaches' Poll to No. 10. After having the week off, they again dropped in the coaches' poll to No. 11. They also slipped from No. 11 to No. 12 in the Associated Press Poll.

"They have said we played two bad teams and then we struggled with Louisville," defensive end Shaq Lawson said. "We pretty much try not to pay attention to that because at the end of the day, if we do our job and execute on the field and win, we are going to move up eventually."

Clemson and its fan base got the respect they were seeking when 82,415 fans sat in a driving rainstorm and watched the Tigers build a 21–3 lead through three quarters. Clemson jumped out to a 14–0 lead right off the bat thanks to a Watson to Jordan Leggett 6-yard touchdown pass on the game's opening drive, which Watson followed up with a 13-yard touchdown pass to wide receiver Artavis Scott on the next possession.

Just 6:17 into the game, the Tigers already owned a two-score lead. Clemson led 14–3 at halftime.

It did not take long for the Tigers to extend the lead to 18 points in the third quarter. On the kickoff, kicker Ammon Lakip stripped C.J. Sanders of the football, and C.J. Fuller recovered it at the Notre Dame 29. On third

Clemson linebacker Ben Boulware stops Notre Dame quarterback DeShone Kizer just short of the goal line in the Tigers' 24–22 victory over the Irish in 2015. The Clemson Insider.

down and 2 from the 21, Watson ran up the middle, broke one would-be tackle and walked into the end zone for a 21–3 advantage.

"Give credit to Clemson. I thought they came out fresh and aggressive and made things difficult for us early on," Notre Dame head coach Brian Kelly said. "Certainly, they carried the play in the first half." But the game was far from over. Kizer was no Joe Montana, but he sure did his best to impersonate him.

Kizer, who threw for 321 yards and two touchdowns, first hit running back C.J. Prosise for a 56-yard touchdown on a wheel route that was perfectly executed down the far sideline.

Following a Greg Huegel 35-yard field goal to extend Clemson's lead to 24–9 with 10:56 to play, Kizer ran 3 yards for a second score and finally found Torii Hunter Jr. for a 1-yard score to pull Notre Dame to within two points with seven seconds to play.

Kizer threw for 202 yards in the fourth quarter on 9-of-12 passing. "I wish we could have supported him better," Kelly said. "I'm really proud of him and the way he competed. He played well enough for us to win."

Clemson finally stopped Kizer on the next play, when Watkins blew through a double team and helped Ben Boulware make the game-winning tackle on the Irish's two-point attempt to tie the game.

For a second straight game, the defense found a way to make one more play at the end. When it was over, an emotional Dabo Swinney delivered one of the best postgame interviews of all time to ABC sideline reporter Heather Cox. "It ain't always perfect. But what I told them tonight was, listen, we give you scholarships. We give you stipends, and meals, and a place to live. We give you nice uniforms. But I can't give you guts. And I can't give you heart. And tonight, hey, it was B.Y.O.G. Bring your own guts. And they brought some guts and some heart, and they never quit 'til the last play."

And luckily, Kizer was not Joe Montana.

17

2015 Was Clemson's Season of Harvest

As the confetti poured onto the field and Alabama celebrated its sixteenth national championship, Clemson quarterback Deshaun Watson walked over to his new friend, Alabama running back Derrick Henry, and congratulated him and the Crimson Tide on a great game.

"We're going to try to link up after the off-season. I want to learn from him and just really build that relationship," Watson said afterward. "He's the Heisman winner, national champion, so I'm trying to do the same thing, and I just want to learn from guys that have been there and have done it."

I doubt Watson had to learn too much. He and the Tigers came so close to winning it all in 2015. Watson set a national championship game record with 478 total yards and threw four touchdown passes in nearly guiding the Tigers past Alabama. "A lot of people thought they were going to pound us, but they didn't," Watson said. "We stood toe-to-toe and it was a four-quarter fistfight. It came down to the last play so we will be motivated. We will learn from this feeling and get ready for next year."

When the 2015 season began, not many imagined that, on January 11, 2016, Clemson was going to play for a championship. And though some in the media may have doubted the Tigers' chances, the guys inside the locker room never did. Watson himself laid out the goal back in fall camp, when he said they could win the national championship.

They bought into Dabo Swinney's "no game is more important than the next one" and rode that in wins over Wofford, App State and Louisville to start the season. Against Notre Dame, in a driving rainstorm, Clemson dominated the lines of scrimmage and had the Irish hoping for a little luck at the end just to push the game into overtime.

The Tigers continued to impress with easy wins over Georgia Tech and Boston College. And then there was the 58-point massacre in Miami. After the Miami game, the rest of the world started to take notice. Clemson was for real.

Back home, Clemson mania was everywhere—on the internet, in the newspapers, on the radio and on the television. The Tigers surged to No. 3 in the polls and everyone started to ask, "Can they really win it all?"

The euphoria of the season rolled along as the Tigers got another big day from Watson while putting up 56 points and more that 600 yards on NC State's top-10 defense. The following week against Florida State, fresh off being ranked No. 1 in the first College Football Playoff Rankings, the Tigers answered all the doubters again and beat the one team they had not been able to take down the last three years.

Clemson was now in cruise control to get to the playoffs.

The excitement from the Clemson fan base was at an all-time high. Though Bank of America Stadium's seats are painted baby blue, they were filled by a record number of fans dressed in orange as Clemson took over Charlotte and the Tigers took home the ACC Championship.

The next day, back in Death Valley, more than thirty thousand fans made it out of bed and joined Swinney and his team at high noon for the world's largest pizza party. The Tigers found out that they were the top seed in the College Football Playoff and would face No. 4 Oklahoma in the Orange Bowl.

When Swinney spoke to the crowd, he said something that stuck out to me. He told the crowd to "enjoy the ride." The Tigers smothered the Sooners in the South Florida heat and advanced to the National Championship Game in Glendale, Arizona.

For a little while, the Tigers had the heavyweight champs on the ropes, but in the end, Alabama made just enough plays to hold off the upstart Tigers, 45–40. But in the Clemson locker room, there was not any crying. There were not any sad faces. To a man, everyone seemed mad. They knew they let a golden opportunity slip by.

But like Swinney said back at the pizza party the month before, more opportunities lay ahead. After quoting from the Bible (Galatians 6:9), Swinney said: "This team has not grown weary. They have stayed the course and they have overcome all kinds of obstacles. What I want you to know is that this is our season of harvest, but it is just getting started."

18

WATSON, TIGERS COMPLETE
THEIR MISSION

When Jalen Hurts raced 30 yards up the middle of the field for a touchdown with 2:07 to play, giving Alabama a three-point lead, Deshaun Watson just smiled.

"They left too much time on the clock," Watson said he thought to himself on the Clemson sideline just before leading the Tigers on a drive for the ages in a 35–31 victory, clinching the program's first national championship since 1981.

ESPN analysts Kirk Herbstreit and Joey Galloway have both said that if there was one game they had to win and they had to pick a quarterback who could go win the game for them, they would both choose Deshaun Watson.

Why?

It's Watson's ability to stay calm under pressure. He never gets lost in the moment. No moment is too big for him.

Such was the case earlier in the season, when the Tigers trailed at Florida State by five points with 3:23 left on the clock. Earlier in the game, Watson had thrown two interceptions and just seemed a little off from his normal self. But when it was crunch time and Clemson needed one last scoring drive, Deshaun was Deshaun. He was not nervous, he was not too high, he was not too low—he was just calm. He was ready to lead his team down the field and get the win.

"He handles adversity better than most other people," Clemson tight end Jordan Leggett said. "He just goes out there and moves on to the next play. He just brings a whole different kind of confidence to the offense and

Deshaun Watson threw for a then-CFP record 420 yards and four touchdowns in Clemson's win over Alabama in the 2017 CFP National Championship. *Clemson Insider.*

helps us play easier, play with calmness. We can just chill and relax and go out there and play.

"It was stressful [being down], but we knew we were going to win no matter what."

Without even blinking, Watson led Clemson on a five-play, 75-yard drive that he capped with a 34-yard touchdown pass to Leggett for the winning score.

"I feel blessed to have the best quarterback in the country. Obviously, the media and other people are going to say certain things. But I believe he is the best player in the country, and he has unbelievable poise and unbelievable knowledge," Clemson co–offensive coordinator Tony Elliott said.

The win in Tallahassee on October 29, 2016, was the third time that season that Watson led the Tigers on a game-winning drive at the end of regulation or overtime. He also threw a winning touchdown pass to Leggett— this time for 31 yards—in Clemson's come-from-behind win over Louisville on October 1 and threw a 10-yard touchdown pass to Artavis Scott to beat NC State in overtime on October 15.

"It honestly does not surprise me," said Michael Perry, Watson's quarterback coach in high school. "He obviously is very talented. God blessed him tremendously, but when you put his talent with that work ethic, that's what makes him what he is. I guarantee you right now, that kid is in his room looking at film. There is no doubt."

Watson has hundreds of thousands of fans, but his biggest fan might reside in Tuscaloosa, Alabama. Crimson Tide head coach Nick Saban, who recruited Watson when he played at Gainesville High School, said prior to the start of the College Football Playoff that if he had input into the Heisman Trophy process, he would have given his vote to the Tigers' star quarterback.

Saban saw firsthand how good of a quarterback Watson is when he is at his best. Watson completed thirty of forty-seven passes for 405 yards and four touchdowns in the 2016 National Championship Game. He also rushed for 73 yards against the Alabama defense, which came in to the contest with the best defense in the country. "I think he is a fantastic competitor and a great player and played a fantastic game against us. I don't get to see him all that much during the season, but I have a tremendous amount of respect for the guy. He did a fabulous job," Saban said.

Though he is a fan, Watson was the last guy Saban wanted to see with the ball in his hands with the national championship on the line.

"Deshaun Watson, I've said this all week long, is probably the most dynamic player in college football, maybe the best player in college football relative to what he does for his team," Saban said in the week leading up to the championship game. "A combination of his ability to pass the ball accurately, execute their offense in the passing game, as well as his physical ability to run the ball and add quarterback runs to their whole system of very good players, whether it's running backs or wide receivers, and he can utilize all the talent on their team because of his skill set."

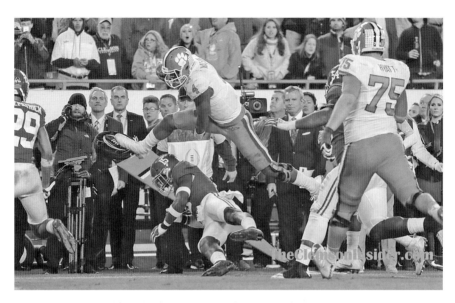

Deshaun Watson hurdles an Alabama defender in the fourth quarter of Clemson's win over the Crimson Tide in the 2017 CFP National Championship. The Clemson Insider.

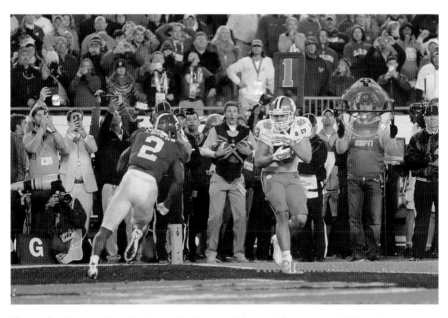

Hunter Renfrow catches the game-winning touchdown with one second left to beat Alabama in the 2017 CFP National Championship. The Clemson Insider.

Saban could not put his finger on just one thing Watson does well, because he does so many things well.

"Sometimes you look at an athletic quarterback, and you think, well, this guy is going to run around and extend plays all the time," the Alabama head coach said. "He does that extremely well when he needs to. But that's not his style of play. He reads the defense. He gets the ball out of his hand quickly. He does a really good job of reading what you're playing on defense and tries to take advantage of it relative to where he needs to go with the ball.

"I think trying to disguise things is important, but I also think not allowing him to extend plays, which is where they made some big plays on us a year ago where the defense breaks down because of his athleticism and then he takes advantage of it."

Michael Perry remembers how calm Watson was on the day he and his Gainesville teammates played Sandy Creek High School in the quarterfinal round of the state playoffs in 2011. Sandy Creek had a forty-one-game winning streak and was the favorite to win another state championship.

Watson was a sophomore, and he did not care. "He just played phenomenal. It was like he was a man amongst boys, and he was just a sophomore going against a state power," Perry said. "They had won 41 games in a row, and he just ends it just like that. He just led us up and down the field."

Watson completed twenty-three of thirty-two passes that night for 169 yards and two touchdowns. He also rushed for 129 yards in the 35–21 victory.

"He was not rattled. He never gets rattled," Perry said.

And that is what makes Watson uncommon among a world of common quarterbacks. "That's why he is such a good quarterback because that's what you have to have. With the quarterback position it can be an up and down roller-coaster, but Deshaun is just as steady as he can be," Perry said.

That was never more obvious than in the national championship game. Here Watson was, down three points to an Alabama team that had won twenty-six straight games, while going against the best defense in the country, 68 yards away from the end zone and with 2:01 showing on the clock.

"We practice two-minute all the time, and we prepare for moments like this all the time," said Watson, who totaled four touchdowns and threw for a championship record 420 yards on thirty-six of fifty-six passes. "We had so many situations throughout the season where we did it before halftime and at the end of the game. So, it was just another opportunity for us to show what we're about, just on a bigger stage."

Ninety-seven times in Nick Saban's career, his teams have entered the fourth quarter with a doubt-digit lead, and all ninety-seven times they walked

Deshaun Watson (*right*) and Carlos Watkins (*left*) celebrate Clemson's 2016 national championship. *The Clemson Insider.*

away with a victory. That was the case in the 2017 national championship game. Thanks to a 68-yard touchdown pass from Hurts to tight end O.J. Howard, the Crimson Tide had a 24–14 lead entering the final quarter.

However, that quickly changed when Watson found Mike Williams in the end zone from four yards out, cutting the lead to three at 24–21 with 14:00 to play.

On Clemson's next possession, it took the lead for the first time, 28–24, as Wayne Gallman went in from 1 yard out to cap a six-play, 88-yard drive that took 1:55 off the clock with 4:38 left in the game.

The lead was short-lived, as Alabama got a great third-down pass from Hurts to ArDarius Stewart. Three plays later, Hurts sprinted into the end zone from 30 yards out, setting up the greatest drive in Clemson history or possibly in the history of college football.

"God put us there for a reason, and we just went out there, and I told the guys, 'Hey, let's be great, let's be special,'" Watson said. "My offensive line gave me time, the receivers made big, big plays, and I just pretty much had the easy part, just getting the ball in the direction of the receivers and let them go out there and make the plays."

Clemson opened "The Drive" with a 5-yard pass to Leggett. On the next play, Watson found Williams, who made a circus-like catch down the left side for 24 yards to the Alabama 39. On the next play, Clemson used a little trickery as Artavis Scott caught a pass and then flipped it backward to running back Wayne Gallman, moving the football to the 33. After a 1-yard run to the 32 by Gallman, Watson hit Hunter Renfrow for a 6-yard gain on third-and-3, moving the ball to the Alabama 26.

With nineteen seconds to go, Watson fired a pass to Leggett's left shoulder as the senior made a twisting grab to snag the ball for a first down at the 19-yard line with fourteen seconds to play. A play later, Williams drew a pass interference penalty in the end zone, placing the ball at the 2-yard line with six seconds to play. "We were not playing for overtime. We were going for the win. That's our mentality," Dabo Swinney said.

Swinney said co–offensive coordinator Jeff Scott, who knew Alabama liked to go to man-to-man coverage when backed inside their 5-yard line, was adamant that Clemson run a rub route, where Artavis Scott cuts inside and tries to get in the way of the defender covering Renfrow, allowing him to break open in the flats.

So, as Watson rolled to his right, Renfrow was wide open for the winning touchdown. "Never in a million years did I think I would catch the game-winning pass," Renfrow said. "It's been such a journey for me. It's like I got knocked out in the third quarter and this was all a dream.

"Credit to—I think my faith in God really got me through it, just passing up the money to go to App State and to come and play for a guy like Coach Swinney, and a quarterback like Deshaun is pretty special."

The whole drive was special. It was just 68 yards, but it meant so much more. Watson said that, even before he threw the game-winner to Renfrow, he just enjoyed the moment and knew what was about to happen. He knew history was being made, and he, along with his Clemson teammates and coaches, were right in the middle of it. "I just kind of slowed down the moment," Watson said. "I just kind of smiled to myself and just knew because I knew that we were inside the five and I knew they were going to play straight cover zero man, and I knew if [Scott] makes his block and get the little pick, Renfrow was going to get in the end zone.

"I kind of smiled, and I knew before I even snapped the ball it was going to be a touchdown. All I had to do was just get the ball to him. I slowed down the moment, everyone made their blocks and did their part, and I did my part, and we pulled it out."

After coming up short in the previous year's title game to Alabama, Clemson's players and coaches made a pact at the start of the 2016 season that if they got back to the championship game, they would do all they could to make sure no one left with any regrets.

Deshaun Watson led Clemson to its first national championship in thirty-five years when he helped the Tigers win the 2016 national title. The Clemson Insider.

When Renfrow caught the game-winner from Watson with one second to go, Clemson had accomplished its mission—they were national champions. "It was an awesome feeling, and it was a great way to finish off the game," Watson said.

19

THE BEST EVER!

After his team debuted as the No. 2 team in the College Football Playoff Committee's initial top 25 poll on October 30, 2018, Dabo Swinney said to ESPN's Rece Davis at the time that his team belonged on the ROY bus with everyone else in the country.

Alabama was already being dubbed the greatest team of all time, especially by those at the four-letter network. The Crimson Tide had all but won the national championship; everyone just wondered who was going to come in second, which is why Clemson's head coach brought up the ROY bus.

ROY was an acronym, meaning "Rest of Y'all," something Swinney derived from his playing days at Alabama, when he was a walk-on.

"The reality of it is, back when I was a player, we kind of had the big-time bus and then the ROY bus—the Rest of Y'all—it is kind of Alabama and the rest of y'all. We are just kind of glad to be on the ROY bus right now and to still have a chance," Swinney said. "But it really does not matter. It is exciting to know that we are getting into November and we are still a team that is in the middle of the hunt."

Davis laughed and said to Swinney that Clemson very much belonged up front with the Crimson Tide, especially the way Clemson was rolling through its competition. The Tigers were coming off a stretch in which they had outscored their last three opponents—Wake Forest, NC State and Florida State—by a score of 163–20.

"Alabama is on the buses one, two and three and we are on the ROY—the Rest of Y'all. We are in that group. The Rest of Y'all," Swinney said while laughing.

Christian Wilkins (42) and Clelin Ferrell (99) returned to Clemson for one more season in 2018 and helped lead the Tigers to their third national championship. The Clemson Insider.

Though Swinney was joking around, his humble approach was very much deliberate. He wanted to keep his team hungry, because he knew there was a good chance the Tigers and Tide were on a collision course to meet in the national championship game for a third time in four years.

Over the next two months, Swinney did not let up on his approach, and neither did the media. Alabama, with Heisman hopeful Tua Tagovailoa at quarterback, continued to be the talk of the season, while Clemson, though separated from the rest of the pack, was still considered inferior to Alabama.

"I will say we are driving the ROY Bus," Swinney said the week before the Tigers and Tide played in the national championship game. "We are definitely the driver, but we have a bus load of people and that Alabama bus, they don't have many folks on that one. They are riding in style, that is for sure."

Heading into the College Football Playoff National Championship, Clemson won twelve of its fourteen games by 20 or more points, including the last nine. In the previous nine games, the Tigers had beat their opposition by an average of 36.1 points.

But few were talking about the Tigers. Instead, they stood in the shadow of Alabama and the mighty SEC and did not let it get to them. They knew in time they would get their opportunity.

Ever since he became Clemson's starting quarterback in Week 5 of the 2018 season, everyone waited for Trevor Lawrence to have a freshman moment.

It was supposed to happen against a ranked NC State team in Week 8. It didn't happen, as the true freshman led the Tigers to a rout of the Wolfpack.

It was supposed to happen at a ranked Boston College team in Week 11. It didn't happen, as Clemson won by 20 points at Chestnut Hill.

It was supposed to happen in the College Football Playoff Semifinals against Notre Dame. But Lawrence diced up the Irish on his way to being named Cotton Bowl MVP.

So, in the week leading up to the national championship game, just about everyone expected Lawrence to have his freshman moment. After all, this is Alabama. This is the King of the SEC. There is no way the Tide is going to let a blond-hair quarterback with a nickname of "Sunshine" beat them.

This is the game for sure that Lawrence will have his freshman moment.

Well, it never happened.

Lawrence was named the MVP of the championship game after he completed twenty of thirty-two passes for 347 yards and three touchdowns in leading the Tigers to a 44–16 victory, winning the program its second national championship in three years. "That doesn't mean as much as being able to be a part of this team," Lawrence said afterward. "Really it's true, even if we didn't go all this way and win a National Championship, this has been a team that I'll never forget for one, and it's just been amazing, the focus and how driven this team is has been unbelievable.

"Just these seniors, just taking me in, and they kind of dragged me along until I got my feet under me, they're awesome people as well as players."

In becoming the first true freshman to win a national championship since 1985, Lawrence completed eight of ten passes for 240 yards on third downs. All three of his touchdown passes came on third down, as did his 62-yard pass to Tee Higgins to set up the Tigers' first offensive score of the night.

"I mean, the games like this you've got to make big plays, and the guys that we have, they definitely did that. You just give them a chance, and they'll come down with it. Like I said about the O-line, same thing about the receivers and running backs and everyone else. Just amazing players and really just so proud of them. It took a lot to get here, but really just proud of those guys."

Trevor Lawrence throws a pass during the Tigers' win over Alabama in the 2019 CFP National Championship. *The Clemson Insider.*

Because of Lawrence, Clemson finished the night with 482 yards and averaged 7.7 yards per play.

"It was just surreal," he said. "So yeah, it was even better. It's always great just to get another game with this group of guys. Like I said, just been an amazing year. But yeah, it was amazing.

"Obviously, our fans were awesome, traveled well. So, thank you all for that. And then yeah, just an unbelievable experience."

Everything seemed to be going well for Alabama at the start of the game. The Tide won the toss and kicked off to Clemson and forced a three-and-out. Then Tagovailoa completed two passes and Bama was on the move with a first down at its own 41.

But what Tagovailoa and Alabama did not know is that Clemson had them right where they wanted them. On the next play, the Tide's All-American quarterback thought the Tigers were in man coverage, so when Isaiah Simmons came on a corner blitz, Tagovailoa thought he was throwing to an open receiver.

Instead, A.J. Terrell was playing zone. Tagovailoa threw the football right to the Clemson corner. The sophomore from Atlanta obliged and took the football 44 yards for a touchdown.

Alabama was stunned, and Clemson had a 7–0 lead. "We thought they would throw the ball to us based on what we were doing with our SAM [strongside linebacker]," Clemson defensive coordinator Brent Venables said. "We were in a cloud coverage, something we really haven't done going into the game and it worked out to perfection."

A lot worked out for the Clemson defense in the national championship game. Though it gave up 443 yards to the Tide, it held them to a season-low 16 points, the fewest ever for a Saban-coached team at Alabama. "Obviously, that is Alabama. They are going to make some plays," Venables said. "I am so proud of those guys for not getting discouraged and to continue to believe in themselves and in each other."

Alabama had its opportunities. On its first three possessions of the second half, it reached the Clemson red zone, only to be turned away each time.

The Tide reached the Clemson 22-, 14- and 2-yard line and failed to get the ball into the end zone or come away with any points.

"To see them go out as champs and as the number one scoring defense in all of football, 15-0, the best ever and the best offense I have been around. To me, they are just a little bit better than Southern Cal's offense in 2004 so whatever that means," Venables said. "This is a special performance and

A.J. Terrell takes back an interception for a touchdown in the first quarter of the Tigers' 44–16 win over Alabama in the 2019 CFP National Championship. Clemson Insider.

a special year. This is a great legacy these guys have lived out and I cannot thank them enough.

"I think your character and your leaderships is revealed in those moments. It is easy to say, but that is what it comes to. It is a sure will to win and compete and not to be discouraged and not be denied and find a way. They epitomized all of those things in those series."

Other than the Tigers' two interceptions on Tagovailoa, the defense also snuffed out an Alabama fake punt after the Tide's opening drive of the third quarter bogged down at the Clemson 22. Nyles Pinckney busted through the line and tackled holder Mac Jones for a loss.

"We stemmed to a Cover 2, which was like no block," Venables said. "We went into the game knowing they would have a fake and we showed one front and steamed to another and played Cover 2 to it and sniffed it out, so it was game plan specific just assuming there might be a critical time in the game where they might be able to seize the momentum and make that play. We always have different field goal fake defenses, but this one was game plan specific and guys executed it to perfection."

The Tigers closed out arguably the greatest single season by a college football team with their thumping of Alabama. "We are the best ever. Until somebody does what we did, go 15-0 and how we did it! We are the best ever," defensive end Austin Bryant said.

Clemson did it, not just against Alabama, but pretty much against everyone. The Tigers trailed in just six games all season, and in all but one, they had control of the game by halftime. The one game was against Syracuse, when Chase Brice came off the bench for an injured Trevor Lawrence and saved the season.

In all, Clemson won thirteen games by at least 20 points. Of those thirteen wins, two were by 60-plus points, the first team in ACC history to have two victories of 60 or more point in the same season. Two other wins were by 41 points or more, while three were by 31 or more points.

"I do not want to disrespect any of the other great teams that came before us. But when you are the first to do something, I feel like you earn a little respect and a little attention," defensive tackle Christian Wilkins said. "But people will probably not want to believe it because we are just a bunch of funky old' Tigers. We are just some funky raggedy old' Tigers from Clemson. This isn't supposed to be us. We are not supposed to be here. These moments and things like this are supposed to be for teams like Alabama, Ohio State and all of those other great programs. I am glad the Tigers were the first ones to be able to get it done."

Dabo Swinney celebrates Clemson's third national championship with cornerback Trayvon Mullen (*right*) and defensive tackle Christian Wilkins following the 2019 CFP National Championship. The Clemson Insider.

Six other victories were by 20-plus points, including a 27-point win over an undefeated Notre Dame team in the Cotton Bowl and then the 28-point beatdown they handed previously undefeated Alabama in the national championship game.

"It speaks for itself. Just hats off to this team and this program," defensive end Clelin Ferrell said. "We feel like we were the best team in college football and, obviously, you have to beat the best to be the best and we went out there and did what we wanted to do and that was put on a dominant performance.

"I feel like it is not really up for debate. We are the best team ever. We're 15-0. The most wins by a senior class and we beat the best team that was considered the best team in the history of college football."

Though the Tigers won their second national title in three years, Ferrell said it is not going to end here. He said 2018 is still just the beginning for this program under Swinney.

"He had a vision for this program and that vision is still formulating," Ferrell said. "This is not the pinnacle. He will tell you right now that this is not the pinnacle. We have twins [two national titles] now, but we want about twelve kids in our family. You know what I mean?

"It is just crazy because he always wants more, and he wants the best for us. It is not about what the players want. It is about what the players need and what this program needs, and he does it the right way. He is always about putting God first and that is what I love about him. He has always made Him the head of his vision, so I love that man to death."

20

Under Swinney, Clemson Is Premier Program in College Football

Though LSU won the 2019 national championship and was the best team in the country that year, it can be argued that Clemson holds the title as the best program in the country.

Clemson's loss to LSU in the 2020 College Football Playoff National Championship was the program's first defeat since the 2017 season, when it lost to Alabama in the 2018 Sugar Bowl. In between, the Tigers won an ACC-tying twenty-nine games in row, which is tied with 2012–14 Florida State, 1990–93 Miami (Florida) and 1901–03 Michigan for the twelfth-longest in FBS history.

Clemson's seniors concluded their careers 55-4 over the last four seasons, tied with the 2018 Clemson and Alabama seniors for the most wins in a four-year career in FBS history.

"These seniors, I'm just so thankful," head coach Dabo Swinney said. "I mean, truly, just God's grace to allow me to watch them develop over the last four and five years, to be with guys like Tanner [Muse], just thankful for them. I'm thankful. No scoreboard changes that. We all hurt. We're all disappointed, but we're not defined by that.

"These guys, they competed with all they had. So sometimes you come up short. Only one team can win, and the best team won tonight. That's just the bottom line. They were the better team tonight. There's nothing you can do but tip your hat and get back to work."

Clemson concluded the 2010s with a record of 117-23 (.836). Clemson's mark in the 2010s represents only the fourth time a program has won 117 games in a decade in major college football since 1890, joining Penn (124 in the 1890s), Alabama (124 in the 2010s) and Ohio State (117 in the 2010s).

Clemson's fourteen wins on the year finish tied for the second-most in school history with the 2015 and 2016 squads.

The Tigers dropped to 6-3 all-time in College Football Playoff games. Clemson's six all-time wins in the playoff remain tied with Alabama for the most in CFP history. No school other than Clemson and Alabama has more than two.

Clemson has won two national championships in the last four years and has played for the title four times in the last five seasons.

"From where we were in 2009, my first year, to where we are now, been in five straight playoffs, and we've won two out of the last four National Championships, and we've been in four National Championships. You know, I think we've got 69 wins in the last five years, which is the most ever in the history of college football over that span," Swinney said. "So, we've built a program of consistency, and that's really what it's about to me, and

Dabo Swinney and South Carolina head coach Will Muschamp speak before the Tigers' win in Columbia in 2019. Clemson entered the 2020 game with a six-game winning streak over the Gamecocks. The Clemson Insider.

One of Clemson's first football games on Bowman Field. *Clemson Athletic Communications.*

it's not just on the field. We've been top 10 academically nine of my 11 years and eight out of the last nine, us, Duke and Northwestern. So, we've had a lot of consistency on the field and a lot of consistency off the field.

"That's truly what to me matters most. We'll have more opportunities. These are tough moments. But when I hang my whistle up, it won't be about these moments. It's not going to be about the confetti flying and winning a National Championship or a very disappointing painful moment like this where you come up short. It's really more about the relationships that you have. That's the true joy, just getting a chance to just come to work every day with such great people. I've got a wonderful staff that are so loyal, so committed, and just a bunch of beautiful young men that lay it on the line."

BIBLIOGRAPHY

Blackman, Sam, and Tim Bourret. *If These Walls Could Talk*. Chicago: Triumph Books, 2016.

Blackman, Sam, Bob Bradley, Chuck Kriese and Will Vandervort. *Clemson: Where the Tigers Play*. New York: Sports Publishing, 2013 and 2017.

Bradley, Bob. *Death Valley Days: The Glory of Clemson Football*. Atlanta, GA: Longstreet Press, 1991.

Sahadi, Lou. *The Clemson Tigers: From 1896 to Glory*. New York: William Morrow & Company, 1983.

Index

About the Author

Will Vandervort has covered Clemson University Athletics for nearly two decades as a sportswriter and editor. He is currently the senior writer for *The Clemson Insider*, an independent website that covers Clemson Athletics and the Atlantic Coast Conference on a daily basis.

Vandervort is an award-winning sportswriter and editor who, before joining TCI in September 2012, worked as the editor for IPTAY Media, which ran the Clemson Athletic Department's outgoing publications to its donors. He covered Clemson University Athletics and wrote for the athletic department's website and newsletter. Vandervort was also an editor for the athletic department's magazine, *Orange: The Experience*.

Besides his duties as an editor and writer, Vandervort was also the cohost of *The Tiger Pregame Show*, a three-hour radio show on Clemson game days that airs on Clemson's flagship station WCCP-FM in Clemson.

Vandervort, who resides in the Clemson area, has been a sportswriter and editor for twenty-three years at newspapers and websites in Georgia and South Carolina. He has covered college football in the ACC and the SEC for most of that time as well as covering some Division II college football and the NFL. Vandervort has covered Clemson University sports since 2004, first as an editor/beat writer for the the Seneca *Journal* and then as the editor for IPTAY Media.